PASTORAL LEADERSHIP:

Shepherding and Caring for God's People

JAMISON J. HARDY

CONCORDIA PUBLISHING HOUSE · SAINT LOUIS

Published by Concordia Publishing House
3558 S. Jefferson Avenue, St. Louis, MO 63118-3968
1-800-325-3040 • cph.org

Manufactured in the United States of America

1 2 3 4 5 6 7 8 9 10 32 31 30 29 28 27 26 25 24 23

Contents

Foreword

The Lutheran Church—Missouri Synod likes to work with "either/or" categories. There is good reason for this when it comes to matters of the faith once delivered to the saints (Jude 3). Either you believe what the Scriptures teach and the Lutheran Confessions affirm about the faith, or you don't. Either you believe that the Holy Trinity is one divine essence in three persons, or you don't. Either you believe that our Lord Christ is truly God and truly man, or you don't. Either you believe that Jesus is *the* way and *the* truth and *the* life, or you don't. These teachings are absolutes. And being exclusive in nature, they not only state what is to be believed but they also condemn, either explicitly or implicitly, those individuals who reject biblical teaching.

That's the way theology, properly speaking, works. At the same time, however, God has allowed us the opportunity to apply biblical and confessional theology in a world that struggles under the reality of human fallenness. In this world and, of course, also within the church, we deal daily with the reality of broken human individuals and skewed human institutions. Luther had such great confidence at the beginning of the Reformation that freeing the Word of God from the shackles of human obfuscation would transform and reform the church into what God had intended for it. But toward the end of his life, his frustration showed itself more and more as his expectations and hopes proved difficult to realize.

Perhaps Luther himself fell into a kind of theology of glory, at least at points in his life. And, of course, we do too. It's always a temptation because we *know* and *believe* the truth and trust in Him. And we want others to *know* and *believe* in Him. But when they don't, or worse, when they reject Him despite the wonderful character of His Gospel, we can become terribly frustrated and even fall into despair. The temptation of a theology of glory is always at hand, and the realization of the Church Triumphant remains out of reach.

And that's why we call our experience now the way of the Church Militant. We struggle daily, personally and corporately, to help realize God's rightly confessing Church as we share the Gospel to a world that desperately needs to hear it. Daily we strive, and daily we fail, even as we recognize this will be the rhythm of our individual and corporate lives. It is our task to recognize that we are Christ's own, even as "the Old Adam in us should by daily contrition and repentance be drowned and die with all sins and evil desires," and, wonderfully, "that a new man should daily emerge and arise to live before God in righteousness and purity forever" (Small Catechism, Baptism, Fourth Part).

It is particularly within the context of our corporate life together outside of the Divine Service—though not apart from it—that Dr. Jamison Hardy's *Pastoral Leadership: Shepherding and Caring for God's People* fills a real need. As Pastor Hardy points out, "A vast majority of what I would do as a pastor was tied up in being a pastoral leader."

In this volume, aimed specifically at pastoral leaders, Pastor Hardy writes from this conviction: pastoral leadership is pastoral care. While it is not, properly speaking, teaching the Gospel purely and administering the Sacraments according to Christ's command (Augsburg Confession VII), it is inseparably bound up with supporting preaching and administration. Pastoral leadership supports the central pastoral acts.

And that is where this volume shines. It offers a fully biblical picture of pastoral leadership, both the joys and the challenges. It is brutally honest, dealing with the very human realities of hesitation and stubbornness, as well as feelings of doubt, guilt, and unworthiness. It emphasizes the importance of good and transparent communication and underscores the necessity of being capable in the arena of finance. It encourages every pastor to invest in future leaders. But, most important of all, it is centered in Christ, the One who "did what He asks us to do." For in the end, as Pastor Hardy explains, Christ is at the center as the One who leads His Church and His pastors in the midst of the challenges that we face together.

This book will prove to be a valuable resource to pastors as they consider their own service in Christ. Its practical application of biblically based principles will pull pastors back to its chapters over the course of their ministries. For that, we can be deeply grateful to a man who carries the title of president and bishop, but most important, pastor.

Lawrence R. Rast Jr., President
Concordia Theological Seminary
Fort Wayne, Indiana

Introduction

When I first became a pastor, visions of preaching, teaching, and visiting God's people were among the few things I saw as responsibilities for the pastoral office. Very quickly after being ordained and installed, I realized that a vast majority of what I would do as a pastor was tied up in being a pastoral leader. This was radically different from my expectations. But God showed me through my laypeople that pastoral leadership is more than simply being present around the church and during events.

This reality became clear before I was even installed as a pastor in my first parish. I had one particularly resolute layman, who at the time was president of the congregation. He came into my office and asked me to make a significant number of phone calls to introduce myself to members of the congregation. At the time, I did not understand why this was so important to him. But I later came to realize that those simple calls were setting the tone for my leadership as the pastor in that congregation. I have since used this example on many occasions with young seminarians to set the pastoral leadership tone within the congregational setting where they will serve. Those simple phone calls not only made people aware that I was their new pastor but they also helped generate excitement among the people of God about the new ministry opportunity in that place where God had placed me. Pastoral leadership had begun even without my knowing.

As surprising as it may seem, I was being shaped as a pastoral leader before I knew what was happening. God was using His own people to teach one of His newest pastors about leadership. In many ways, I was totally ignorant of what God was doing to me through the people He had given me to lead and serve. This only became clear to me years later as I began to see marks of leadership shape my pastoral life. Little by little, the leader God intended me to become began to emerge and blossom. Without doing anything on my part, I was being formed as a pastoral leader and servant of the Church. And it was all God's work.

This leadership formation continued throughout my early pastoral years as I watched fellow brothers in the ministry. While I simply put my head down and went to the task of serving God's people, I did not know what was happening within me as I began to emulate the leadership qualities of those men who were within my circle of influence. I subconsciously registered the successful ways these pastors handled leadership situations within the life of the parishes they served, and I started to utilize those very techniques in my parish. My leadership style and manner were already deeply developed and solidified long before I would ever realize what had happened. Thankfully, I had very good mentors and examples throughout my early ministry career, helping to shape and mold me. This was solely by the grace and mercy of our God.

From the very onset of this book, I want to make it absolutely clear that pastoral leadership and pastoral care in most respects are one and the same. Being a leader is not separate from being a pastor. In fact, being a pastoral leader is what God calls us to do when it comes to shepherding His flock and caring for His people. Pastoral care and leadership are not in competition with each other in the Office of the Holy Ministry. Far too often in my life as a district president, I have seen pastors on both sides of this discussion take vastly different approaches, pitting pastoral leadership against pastoral care. There is no question in my mind that pastoral leadership begins and is dominated by preaching the Word of God, administering the Sacraments of Christ properly, and faithfully witnessing the message of Jesus Christ. These are the key and significant elements of both pastoral care and pastoral leadership.

There will be a worldly tension that exists when it comes to the conversation around pastoral leadership. Inevitably, our church confession regarding the Office of the Holy Ministry will be placed side by side with the conversation of pastoral leadership. In no way are these two topics in opposition. Those carrying out the Office of the Holy Ministry as ordained clergymen within this conversation are held to the same confessional standards as a pastoral leader. In the rite of ordination, the pastor makes his vows "in the presence of this congregation and before our Lord God to whom you must give an account now and at the Last Day" (*LSB Agenda*, p. 178). All pastors confess and commit to the principles of ordination—to care for the people of God, to hear confessions and forgive the sins of the penitent, and to teach and preach.

In more than twenty years of ministry, I have seen a clear dividing line between high-quality pastoral leaders and those who are simply carrying out the office. One specific hallmark of being a strong pastoral leader is being present and truly engaged. Being present is not simply about your body in the building or at a meeting, it is about being engaged and committed to what is going on in an authentic way that signals to people that you care. Presence as a pastoral leader is the foundational principle for success throughout the life and ministry of a man. Being present also requires one to be active and interested in what is going on throughout the life of the ministry and the parish in a physical manner. Throughout my experience as a district president, I have clearly seen this lived out in the life of pastors I have served.

It is important to note here that the laity pay attention to what their pastor does in terms of his physical presence in the ministry. One of the greatest complaints I get from lay leaders in congregations today centers around their pastor's lack of presence in ministry outside of Sunday morning. Likewise, I hear pastors talking about the high demand for time away from their families. The simple truth is this: if you are doing your job as a high-quality pastoral leader, there will come moments in your ministry where your family is not the priority as you take care of the people of God. That being said, you should not allow your parish responsibilities to completely take over your life, forcing your family to be neglected and ignored. This can be a temptation, especially at the beginning of your ministry. While this is normal and natural at the onset of any new job or function, you must understand the clear balance that is needed for both high-quality engagements and caring for your family.

This leads to a brief comment on time management. Among many other things that make up a high-quality pastoral leader, I believe time management is up there at the top. There is no doubt in my mind that many of the conflicts I have witnessed as a district president are fueled by either a lack of time management that leads to not spending enough time in the parish, or a lack of time management that leads to spending way too much time in the parish, away from the family. In either of these two cases, it is clear to me that time management can be an enormous distraction in the life of a pastoral leader. Misappropriation of time will always lead to difficulty and disruption for the congregation or the family. Clearly, there is a delicate balance that must always be evaluated and maintained.

Time management can be a difficulty and a struggle for anyone, especially a high-quality pastoral leader. Making sure that you have the right and correct balance of family, personal, and work time will likely be one of the greatest challenges you will encounter. It is crucial for pastoral leaders to remember the proper order of priorities in life—God, family, church. This is the proper order for all Christians, but it is especially important in the life of a high-quality pastoral leader. Without adherence to this order, dysfunction and distractions will always become evident and dominant.

It is not a secret that many of us learn by the example of others. Children watch their fathers and mothers, students watch their teachers, and athletes watch their coaches. In all these cases, positive role modeling affects future outcomes for those who are learning. I have had the pleasure of working with many people who provided me with examples of phenomenal pastoral, corporate, and social leadership. Within the church, good leadership habits simply rubbed off on me as I watched and learned about successful leaders and the ways they carried themselves. Placing myself around people who had a proven record of being effective leaders was something that came naturally to me. I found myself in Rotary, at athletic events, and in social settings, wanting to digest and learn from the best that was around me.

In my early ministry at Our Savior Lutheran Church in Mount Lebanon, Pennsylvania, I was introduced to a men's ministry that included professional athletes from the Pittsburgh Steelers. It was there I first met my favorite Detroit Lion, Jeff Hartings, who had recently been traded to the Pittsburgh Steelers. The young boy in me was giddy as I walked into the men's breakfast and met Jeff. I remember to this day the topic that morning. It was about the biblical concept of iron sharpening iron. That morning was the first time I was exposed to this biblical concept. High-quality biblical leaders setting the example for other biblical leaders to follow is a scriptural principle that we will dive into later in this book. The idea of iron sharpening iron is one that we must unpack further and in more detail. Without both elements of iron in this situation, sharpening cannot occur or have an effect. We need each other.

One of the reasons that I had a desire to author a book on pastoral leadership was born out of my experience as a district president. I have seen the gap that many of my pastors have when it comes to leadership within their congregations. This is not to say in any way that these men are bad pastors. I have simply witnessed many occasions where leadership principles were not at the forefront of decision-making when it came to pastoral leadership. It is true that a pastor has a tremendous influence on his people. Sometimes that influence is based on simple trust and respect for the Office of the Holy Ministry that we inhabit for a brief time. In other cases, pastors gain that influence by demonstrating their ability to be wise and effective pastoral leaders, giving way to laymen and women who have deference for the leadership that their pastor provides within the congregational setting.

My hope is that this book will provide some foundational principles for those who have not had great leadership examples in the past, and that it will give others the tools they need to sharpen and hone their skills to become even more effective pastoral leaders. Throughout the book, I will attempt to cover many topics connected to pastoral leadership. The intention is to bring awareness and clarity to some fundamental leadership topics that seminary education simply does not have time to cover within the curriculum. Some of those topics include fundamental financial vocabulary and understanding, difficult areas that pastors will find themselves in; leading, not following, as a pastoral leader; uplifting others to be leaders; and finally, the connection between leadership and pastoral care. I pray these basic principles will aid and support the reader in applying solid pastoral leadership skills to promote the Gospel and share the love of Christ with all people.

My vocation as bishop and president of the English District has brought a new perspective to my view of pastoral leadership. Many of the things that I will discuss within this book are not new to me; I have thought about them for many years. My role as bishop has enlightened me as to various weaknesses that pastors can face within the parish. Because the Office of the Holy Ministry is always in the public eye, I have noticed that some pastors tend to withdraw from their pastoral leadership initiatives rather than push forward. Perhaps, understandably, they do not want the attention. But high-quality pastoral leaders know that being in the public eye is not only a part of pastoral leadership but, in many respects, it is also the essence of pastoral leadership. Because pastoral leadership is so visible, I believe it also can become extremely intimidating for those who don't understand its importance.

My hope and my prayer is that as you read this book, you will gain knowledge and understanding of the life of a pastoral leader. As you are exposed to different and potentially new situations and concepts, I hope your toolbox of techniques can be filled and used later in ministry and life. Finally, I pray that the Lord enlightens you with His grace and mercies toward being effective and efficient for the sake of the Gospel and the expansion of His kingdom. We fix our eyes on the author of our faith and submit to the will of our God in heaven. After all, there is not a greater example of a faithful and dedicated leader than Christ alone. As Jesus shows in His life and ministry, He always places a greater emphasis on those He serves rather than Himself. As you read this book, I ask you to keep your eyes on the ones you serve rather than on yourself. Developing effective leadership strategies and techniques is always and only in hopes of serving God's people better. For the glory of Christ, we move forward and lead by His grace.

CHAPTER I

Leadership Styles from Biblical Figures

For many people, especially those who are in leadership, self-confidence and courage can be a great struggle. This is not abnormal when it comes to being responsible for an organization or a group of people. It certainly is not unique to our current situation or environment within the church or society. Some of the most effective leaders throughout history have struggled with confidence and self-assurance. For pastors, it is much easier to simply declare and rely on the mercy and love of God to lead a congregation. Satan has patience and a limitless drive to cause faithful people to doubt their ability or their calling from God. This is especially true when it comes to seeing your deficiencies in life and leadership. If a pastor is not already aware of his shortcomings, I can promise you that his people will tell him about those shortcomings frequently.

Throughout the Bible, many biblical figures demonstrate the true humanity of leaders. There are varying and different degrees of leadership struggles that occur within the hearts and minds of those God has chosen to lead. I will detail several prominent biblical figures and the struggles they had while in their leadership positions. I will also attempt to lay out many of the leadership pitfalls that biblical leaders have fallen into and highlight areas to pay attention to and watch out for as you lead God's people. This is meant to help you fashion and shape a complete understanding of what being a leader is all about, and to help you be strong and courageous if you find yourself having some of these same struggles and shortcomings.

Adam and Blame

I would like to begin from the very first interchange in the Book of Genesis with the first man, Adam. In 1 Timothy 2:14, Paul makes it clear that Adam was not deceived by the serpent's lie to Eve. He should have exercised his dominion over the serpent and exposed the lie to protect Eve. Instead, he stood by passively, then ate the fruit himself when Eve handed it to him. When confronted by God with his sin, Adam immediately blamed God and the woman God had given him. His first response to God's question regarding who told him he was naked was to point the finger to others.

> **And they heard the sound of the Lord God walking in the garden in the cool of the day, and the man and his wife hid themselves from the presence of the Lord God among the trees of the garden. But the Lord God called to the man and said to him, "Where are you?" And he said, "I heard the sound of You in the garden, and I was afraid, because I was naked, and I hid myself." He said, "Who told you that you were naked? Have you eaten of the tree of which I commanded you not to eat?" The man said, "The woman whom You gave to be with me, she gave me fruit of the tree, and I ate." (*Genesis 3:8–12*)**

Adam employed the now classic response for being caught in a failure, especially a failure of leadership. His immediate response to the Lord God was, "The woman whom You gave to be with me, she gave me fruit of the tree, and I ate" (v. 12). There was no hesitation in his reaction. He immediately turned the blame on both God and Eve for his failure and transgression in the leadership position in which God had placed him. As head of the household and husband of the family, he was to be the protector and to enforce the rules and laws of God. Immediately upon his failure, his focus turned to defending himself and blaming others.

This is a classic example of a biblical leader who, when confronted with his failure, turned on God and his wife. Fear of failure and fear of inadequacy as a leader can cause many to forsake their roles and responsibilities as given by the Lord God. Adam begins our leadership examples by showing how the greatest biblical leaders struggled with blame and obedience to God. This is why those in leadership should always remain vigilant and on guard, reminding themselves of these biblical examples so as not to fall prey to their temptations also. There will come many times in your role as a leader that you will be tempted to pull what I like to call the Adam card. Satan causes us all to blame others when we are caught in our sins. Serving God and the Church is a difficult task on our best days, and Satan would have us consistently blame others for our failings and the failings of our organizations.

Be aware of Satan's schemes, and be prepared to resist the temptation to blame others when you fail in leadership. Do not feel compelled to point the finger when you have made the mistake. Stand firm in your repentant heart and know that forgiveness is yours in Christ Jesus. Be accountable and know that all great leaders will, from time to time, fail in their responsibilities before God.

Moses and Doubt and Fear

Without a doubt, Moses is one of my favorite Old Testament characters in the Bible. Throughout the biblical text, he gives us many examples of how we should and should not be leading the people of God. Moses provides us a clear picture of someone who was raised in the highest court in the land of Egypt to be a winsome and phenomenal leader. No expense was spared in preparing and training him to be the next pharaoh in Egypt. He was gifted and desired by many to be an associate and friend. And yet he, too, had moments of doubt and fear when God called him into service in His kingdom for His purposes.

> Now Moses was keeping the flock of his father-in-law, Jethro, the priest of Midian, and he led his flock to the west side of the wilderness and came to Horeb, the mountain of God. And the angel of the LORD appeared

> to him in a flame of fire out of the midst of a bush. He looked, and behold, the bush was burning, yet it was not consumed. And Moses said, "I will turn aside to see this great sight, why the bush is not burned." When the Lord saw that he turned aside to see, God called to him out of the bush, "Moses, Moses!" And he said, "Here I am." Then He said, "Do not come near; take your sandals off your feet, for the place on which you are standing is holy ground." And He said, "I am the God of your father, the God of Abraham, the God of Isaac, and the God of Jacob." And Moses hid his face, for he was afraid to look at God.
>
> Then the Lord said, "I have surely seen the affliction of My people who are in Egypt and have heard their cry because of their taskmasters. I know their sufferings, and I have come down to deliver them out of the hand of the Egyptians and to bring them up out of that land to a good and broad land, a land flowing with milk and honey, to the place of the Canaanites, the Hittites, the Amorites, the Perizzites, the Hivites, and the Jebusites. And now, behold, the cry of the people of Israel has come to Me, and I have also seen the oppression with which the Egyptians oppress them. Come, I will send you to Pharaoh that you may bring My people, the children of Israel, out of Egypt." But Moses said to God, "Who am I that I should go to Pharaoh and bring the children of Israel out of Egypt?" He said, "But I will be with you, and this shall be the sign for you, that I have sent you: when you have brought the people out of Egypt, you shall serve God on this mountain." (*Exodus 3:1–12*)

This account demonstrates to us that even the greatest of biblical characters such as Moses can be afraid and have doubt. At times in the life of any pastoral leader, he can feel unqualified to be a leader before the Lord God, like Moses. Moses told God, "Who am I that I should go to Pharaoh and bring the children of

Israel out of Egypt?" (v. 11). There have been times throughout my ministry when I have felt like Moses before God, asking the question, "Who am I that I should serve the Lord?"

This is the great temptation of Satan to cause us to doubt God's plan and His will in our lives. In the case of Moses, as well as with all pastoral leaders, we are called by one greater than ourselves. In Exodus 3:14, God said to Moses, "I am who I am." And He said, "Say this to the people of Israel: 'I am has sent me to you.'" The mighty hand of the Lord God was with Moses even in doubt and fear. Moses was called by God to serve Him according to His will and His way. And so are pastoral leaders.

It is only by faith and trust in God that we can move forward as pastoral leaders with the confidence needed to be effective in the ministry. Like Moses, we must humble ourselves before the Lord to trust that He will provide us with all that we need to carry out His will and His work faithfully. In the life of Moses, God provided his brother Aaron to supplement his deficiencies. And God will provide all that you need in service to Him and leadership toward His people. We, too, must understand God's calling in our life and submit to His will, firmly believing that He will not forsake us.

Gideon and Hesitation

Biblical history has shown that God often uses the most unlikely people to carry out His work and His mission. This was evident in the calling of Gideon to the service of God. Gideon had great hesitation and equally great fear when it came to performing the functions of leadership to which the Angel of the Lord called him.

> Now the angel of the Lord came and sat under the terebinth at Ophrah, which belonged to Joash the Abiezrite, while his son Gideon was beating out wheat in the winepress to hide it from the Midianites. And the angel of the Lord appeared to him and said to him, "The Lord is with you, O mighty man of valor." And Gideon said to him, "Please, my lord, if the Lord is with us, why then has all this happened to us? And

> where are all His wonderful deeds that our fathers recounted to us, saying, 'Did not the LORD bring us up from Egypt?' But now the LORD has forsaken us and given us into the hand of Midian." And the LORD turned to him and said, "Go in this might of yours and save Israel from the hand of Midian; do not I send you?" And he said to Him, "Please, Lord, how can I save Israel? Behold, my clan is the weakest in Manasseh, and I am the least in my father's house." And the LORD said to him, "But I will be with you, and you shall strike the Midianites as one man." (*Judges 6:11–16*)

It is so evident in Gideon's response to the Angel of the Lord how he felt. "Please, Lord, how can I save Israel? Behold, my clan is the weakest in Manasseh, and I am the least in my father's house" (v. 15). His doubt and fear collided, causing him to make excuses for why he could not possibly become the leader God had called him to be. He was not focused on the power and will of God but rather on his meekness and lowliness within the twelve-tribe structure.

This becomes a common theme throughout biblical history. Like Adam and Moses before him, Gideon immediately turned to excuses and fear when God called him to be a leader in His Church. His focus was not on the power and light God had, but on his weakness and shortcomings. He was not concerned with God's promises, but rather was concerned about what he felt was most important. Ironically, God's response to Gideon was not hesitant at all. It was swift and strong when He stated, "But I will be with you, and you shall strike the Midianites as one man" (v. 16).

With this declaration from God, Gideon was reassured that the promises of God and His mighty hand would rest upon him. The calling and story of Gideon is a clear example of how our fears and lack of confidence are overcome by God's power, might, and strength. That old biblical adage rings true in this example. Where we are weak, He is strong. This is the message that Gideon heard in the Old Testament Book of Judges as the Angel of the Lord came and called him into service. Even though Gideon was afraid and hesitant, God provided all that he needed to be an effective servant in the Lord's kingdom. For God simply declared these words, "I will be with you."

David and Guilt

In our next example, David, we move away from feelings of hesitancy, inadequacy, and blame to guilt and overconfidence. David came into leadership with a great deal of confidence from a young age, having had the hand of God rest on him. His confidence turned into sinfulness as he sought that which was not his. He used his influence and position to take something from another that did not belong to him. This grievous sin caused David great lamenting, torment, and anguish as he faced his failings before God, as we hear clearly in Psalm 51:

> Have mercy on me, O God, according to Your steadfast love; according to Your abundant mercy blot out my transgressions. Wash me thoroughly from my iniquity, and cleanse me from my sin!
>
> For I know my transgressions, and my sin is ever before me. Against You, You only, have I sinned and done what is evil in Your sight, so that You may be justified in Your words and blameless in Your judgment. Behold, I was brought forth in iniquity, and in sin did my mother conceive me. Behold, You delight in truth in the inward being, and You teach me wisdom in the secret heart.
>
> Purge me with hyssop, and I shall be clean; wash me, and I shall be whiter than snow. Let me hear joy and gladness; let the bones that You have broken rejoice. Hide Your face from my sins, and blot out all my iniquities. Create in me a clean heart, O God, and renew a right spirit within me. Cast me not away from Your presence, and take not Your Holy Spirit from me. Restore to me the joy of Your salvation, and uphold me with a willing spirit.
>
> Then I will teach transgressors Your ways, and sinners will return to You. Deliver me from bloodguiltiness,

> O God, O God of my salvation, and my tongue will sing aloud of Your righteousness. O Lord, open my lips, and my mouth will declare Your praise. For You will not delight in sacrifice, or I would give it; You will not be pleased with a burnt offering. The sacrifices of God are a broken spirit; a broken and contrite heart, O God, You will not despise.
>
> Do good to Zion in Your good pleasure; build up the walls of Jerusalem; then will You delight in right sacrifices, in burnt offerings and whole burnt offerings; then bulls will be offered on Your altar.

David, like many pastoral leaders today, became overconfident and then arrogant. His influence and power had grown so large that he felt untouchable. He believed that he owed his heart its desires, even if those desires were against God's commands. David's transgression with Bathsheba set the stage for Psalm 51. When the prophet Nathan confronted David and showed him through a story that he was the perpetrator and thief, David confessed and demonstrated sorrow. He declared this in Psalm 51:3, "For I know my transgressions, and my sin is ever before me." It's a matter that is before any leader. Our failings and sins against God can be so overwhelming that they cover our eyes and turn our faces away from the grace and mercy of God.

Even in the shame and disgrace of his own personal sin, David still understood the might and power of his God. As he declares in verse 7, "Purge me with hyssop, and I shall be clean; wash me, and I shall be whiter than snow." David recognized not only that he needed God but also that God had the power to cleanse him and make him whole once again. This example of David is one that any leader should remember and never forget. Becoming overconfident and power-hungry can be used against the biblical leader.

Like David, no one wants to look in the mirror and see the sinful disgrace that is our human condition. Likewise, we don't need to add to our sinful state for God's mercy and grace to be bestowed upon us. This example shows clearly that the hand of God is on the biblical leader in his calling as well as in his forgiveness. If a pastoral leader cannot accept forgiveness by the same means of the blood of Christ as those he serves, then the message that he brings is null and void.

Jonah and Stubbornness

Throughout my ministry as a parish pastor and a district president, my stubbornness has gotten in the way of being an effective and efficient pastoral leader. Jonah is one of the greatest examples in the biblical text of stubbornness and denial of God's will in the life of one of His servants. As a young boy, I remember my pastor telling a member of the congregation who was in his thirties, "You can run from God, but you cannot hide from His calling." This was all centered around my pastor's strong feeling that this man was being called by God to become a pastor. Five years later, this man enrolled in the seminary and is an effective and dedicated pastor to this very day.

The story of Jonah is well known to many within the church and has become a story that defines our obedience to God's will when it comes to our service in His kingdom. This is seen in the account in Jonah 1:

> Now the word of the LORD came to Jonah the son of Amittai, saying, "Arise, go to Nineveh, that great city, and call out against it, for their evil has come up before Me." But Jonah rose to flee to Tarshish from the presence of the LORD. He went down to Joppa and found a ship going to Tarshish. So he paid the fare and went down into it, to go with them to Tarshish, away from the presence of the LORD.
>
> But the LORD hurled a great wind upon the sea, and there was a mighty tempest on the sea, so that the ship threatened to break up. Then the mariners were afraid, and each cried out to his god. And they hurled the cargo that was in the ship into the sea to lighten it for them. But Jonah had gone down into the inner part of the ship and had lain down and was fast asleep.

So the captain came and said to him, "What do you mean, you sleeper? Arise, call out to your god! Perhaps the god will give a thought to us, that we may not perish."

And they said to one another, "Come, let us cast lots, that we may know on whose account this evil has come upon us." So they cast lots, and the lot fell on Jonah. Then they said to him, "Tell us on whose account this evil has come upon us. What is your occupation? And where do you come from? What is your country? And of what people are you?" And he said to them, "I am a Hebrew, and I fear the LORD, the God of heaven, who made the sea and the dry land." Then the men were exceedingly afraid and said to him, "What is this that you have done!" For the men knew that he was fleeing from the presence of the LORD, because he had told them.

Then they said to him, "What shall we do to you, that the sea may quiet down for us?" For the sea grew more and more tempestuous. He said to them, "Pick me up and hurl me into the sea; then the sea will quiet down for you, for I know it is because of me that this great tempest has come upon you." Nevertheless, the men rowed hard to get back to dry land, but they could not, for the sea grew more and more tempestuous against them. Therefore they called out to the LORD, "O LORD, let us not perish for this man's life, and lay not on us innocent blood, for You, O LORD, have done as it pleased You." So they picked up Jonah and hurled him into the sea, and the sea ceased from its raging. Then the men feared the LORD exceedingly, and they offered a sacrifice to the LORD and made vows.

And the LORD appointed a great fish to swallow up Jonah. And Jonah was in the belly of the fish three days and three nights.

Hearing the story of Jonah evokes in many the understanding that you cannot run from God. Jonah 1:3 clearly states, "But Jonah rose to flee to Tarshish from the presence of the LORD." His fleeing from God affected not only him but also all those who were in the boat with him. Jonah's stubbornness to deny God's calling almost cost him his life—and it almost cost the mariners theirs.

After Jonah was thrown into the water, the seas calmed and the people in the boat were safe once again. God's wrath had been settled. His plan was then enacted, as we hear in verse 17, "And the LORD appointed a great fish to swallow up Jonah. And Jonah was in the belly of the fish three days and three nights." While Jonah tried to elude God's call and his stubbornness overcame him, the Lord God in His wisdom and might used the great fish to move Jonah to go where He wanted him to serve.

Jonah did not want to go to Nineveh, yet God had a purpose and a calling for him. Despite Jonah's stubbornness, God carried out His will and His plan. Much like in the story of Jonah, we, too, are faced with the knowledge that God's will is indeed done in our lives and in the life of the Church. We are reminded to be open to the calling of God and to His will in our life, lest a large fish swallow you and spit you on the shore somewhere. Don't let stubbornness cause you to remove yourself from service to God and the Church.

Elijah and Discouragement

Moments occur during pastoral leadership that can be very discouraging for any leader. The sinful condition that people live in can hinder the best leader and cause great frustration and discouragement. Throughout my career, I have had many instances where I have tried to follow biblical mandates clearly and concisely, such as the mandates regarding conflict. But ultimately, I have often gotten frustrated in situations where a God-pleasing outcome did not occur. In one case, I had tried hard to follow Matthew 18 and go directly to my brother to discuss the transgression that he had inflicted on me, and it did not go well. Situations like this have caused me to be discouraged, and I have focused solely on my efforts to fix things rather than on the will of God. This reminds us of the story of Elijah in 1 Kings 19:1–18:

> Ahab told Jezebel all that Elijah had done, and how he had killed all the prophets with the sword. Then Jezebel sent a messenger to Elijah, saying, "So may the gods do to me and more also, if I do not make your life as the life of one of them by this time tomorrow." Then he was afraid, and he arose and ran for his life and came to Beersheba, which belongs to Judah, and left his servant there.
>
> But he himself went a day's journey into the wilderness and came and sat down under a broom tree. And he asked that he might die, saying, "It is enough; now, O LORD, take away my life, for I am no better than my fathers." And he lay down and slept under a broom tree. And behold, an angel touched him and said to him, "Arise and eat." And he looked, and behold, there was at his head a cake baked on hot stones and a jar of water. And he ate and drank and lay down again. And the angel of the LORD came again a second time and touched him and said, "Arise and eat, for the journey is too great for you." And he arose and ate and drank, and went in the strength of that food forty days and forty nights to Horeb, the mount of God.
>
> There he came to a cave and lodged in it. And behold, the word of the LORD came to him, and He said to him, "What are you doing here, Elijah?" He said, "I have been very jealous for the LORD, the God of hosts. For the people of Israel have forsaken Your covenant, thrown down Your altars, and killed Your prophets with the sword, and I, even I only, am left, and they seek my life, to take it away." And He said, "Go out and stand on the mount before the LORD." And behold, the LORD passed by, and a great and strong wind tore the mountains and broke in pieces the rocks before the LORD, but the LORD was not in the wind. And after

> the wind an earthquake, but the LORD was not in the earthquake. And after the earthquake a fire, but the LORD was not in the fire. And after the fire the sound of a low whisper. And when Elijah heard it, he wrapped his face in his cloak and went out and stood at the entrance of the cave. And behold, there came a voice to him and said, "What are you doing here, Elijah?" He said, "I have been very jealous for the LORD, the God of hosts. For the people of Israel have forsaken Your covenant, thrown down Your altars, and killed Your prophets with the sword, and I, even I only, am left, and they seek my life, to take it away." And the LORD said to him, "Go, return on your way to the wilderness of Damascus. And when you arrive, you shall anoint Hazael to be king over Syria. And Jehu the son of Nimshi you shall anoint to be king over Israel, and Elisha the son of Shaphat of Abel-meholah you shall anoint to be prophet in your place. And the one who escapes from the sword of Hazael shall Jehu put to death, and the one who escapes from the sword of Jehu shall Elisha put to death. Yet I will leave seven thousand in Israel, all the knees that have not bowed to Baal, and every mouth that has not kissed him."

Elijah found himself being completely discouraged and looking into the face of sinfulness and failure. He cried aloud to the Lord in verse 4, "It is enough; now, O LORD, take away my life, for I am no better than my fathers." In Elijah's mind, it would have been better for his life to be taken than for him to continue. His discouragement had become so great that he simply wanted out of the leadership position in which he had been placed.

I have witnessed this phenomenon repeatedly during my life as a district president. I have seen very good, faithful pastors overcome with a discouraged heart as they seek to do the will of God in the place where they serve. In almost every case, I have witnessed these men extend themselves in pastoral leadership and not see a return on their efforts or investment of time. This ultimately caused them to simply want to stop serving. Some of my dearest friends have struggled with this, and I have found myself trying to encourage them and lift them up as they work through frustration and disappointment.

In almost every case, in my experience, discouragement is the single greatest tactic that Satan uses to distract the pastoral leader from the work at hand. Like Elijah, most high-quality pastoral leaders experience moments when frustration overtakes them. In Elijah's darkest hour, God spoke into that frustration and discouragement with the word of the Gospel, saying, "Yet I will leave seven thousand in Israel, all the knees that have not bowed to Baal, and every mouth that has not kissed him" (v. 18). He speaks the same Gospel to us today. The promises of God do not fail, and He is with us always throughout any difficulty, trial, or temptation.

Resist the temptation to be discouraged that Elijah faced. Fight the feeling of inadequacy that Satan would lay upon you as you serve God in the Church. The Word of God is sure and true; He will not forsake His children and will lead them on the path that He has called them to serve. Do not lose heart, and trust that God is with you despite the temptations of Satan and the assaults of this world.

Isaiah and Unworthiness

Throughout Isaiah's life and ministry, he had periods where he felt unworthy to serve in the capacity that God had set before him. Isaiah was the great Old Testament prophet who proclaimed the coming of the Messiah, who prophesied of the virgin birth, and who was the mouthpiece of the highest. And still, Satan made him feel unworthy to serve in the post to which God had called him. Despite the impact he had on the Old Testament and the Church at large, Isaiah's feelings of unworthiness were strong. Here is this account from Isaiah 6:1–7:

> In the year that King Uzziah died I saw the Lord sitting upon a throne, high and lifted up; and the train of His robe filled the temple. Above Him stood the seraphim. Each had six wings: with two he covered his face, and with two he covered his feet, and with two he flew. And one called to another and said:

> "Holy, holy, holy is the Lord of hosts; the whole earth is full of His glory!"
>
> And the foundations of the thresholds shook at the voice of him who called, and the house was filled with smoke. And I said: "Woe is me! For I am lost; for I am a man of unclean lips, and I dwell in the midst of a people of unclean lips; for my eyes have seen the King, the Lord of hosts!"
>
> Then one of the seraphim flew to me, having in his hand a burning coal that he had taken with tongs from the altar. And he touched my mouth and said: "Behold, this has touched your lips; your guilt is taken away, and your sin atoned for."

This is a case where God's calling was met with a spirit of unworthiness in Isaiah, a spirit created by Satan's temptation. His lament and his torments were enormous and caused him to cry in verse 5, "Woe is me! For I am lost; for I am a man of unclean lips, and I dwell in the midst of a people of unclean lips." Despite this lament of Isaiah regarding his unworthiness, God's mercy and calling for him were never stronger. We hear in verse 7, "Behold, this has touched your lips; your guilt is taken away, and your sin atoned for." God's loving care for Isaiah was bestowed clearly in His mercy and His forgiveness of sins.

Anyone who serves in the Office of the Holy Ministry as the mouthpiece of God should always remember this passage and be reinvigorated with the Gospel message. The Angel of the Lord carried out God's mercy by placing the burning coal on Isaiah's lips to take away his sin and atone for his failures. This reminded Isaiah, and reminds us today, that the work of salvation and forgiveness is done by God and not by men. This is most similar to the blessed gift of the Lord's Supper, when the body and blood of Jesus touch the lips of the sinful pastor and cleanse him from his sin.

Throughout the earthly ministry of most pastors, there will be periods where we all feel unworthy. It is critical for us to hear the same Gospel message that we preach every week to the people of God as it applies to ourselves. Simply put, your guilt is taken away and your sin is atoned for by the work of Christ Jesus, the Son of God. As a pastoral leader, you proclaim this good news to all.

Peter and Overconfidence

It can be very easy for anyone serving in the office of a pastoral leader to become overconfident and to think more highly of himself than he ought. This is a lesson that every pastoral leader must learn and understand as he matures in his office. Throughout my career, I have witnessed many faithful, loving laymen and women defer to the office despite the reality that I as a sinner was standing in the office at the time. Their view of the Office of the Holy Ministry is so high that anyone filling it is given deference and care. This reality can cause a false sense of pride and lead to overconfidence for anyone.

Peter struggled with this, as Matthew 26:26–46 makes clear:

> Now as they were eating, Jesus took bread, and after blessing it broke it and gave it to the disciples, and said, "Take, eat; this is My body." And He took a cup, and when He had given thanks He gave it to them, saying, "Drink of it, all of you, for this is My blood of the covenant, which is poured out for many for the forgiveness of sins. I tell you I will not drink again of this fruit of the vine until that day when I drink it new with you in My Father's kingdom."
>
> And when they had sung a hymn, they went out to the Mount of Olives. Then Jesus said to them, "You will all fall away because of Me this night. For it is written, 'I will strike the shepherd, and the sheep of the flock will be scattered.' But after I am raised up, I will go before you to Galilee." Peter answered Him, "Though they all fall away because of You, I will never fall away." Jesus said to him, "Truly, I tell you, this very night, before the rooster crows, you will deny Me three times." Peter said to Him, "Even if I must die with You, I will not

> deny You!" And all the disciples said the same.
>
> Then Jesus went with them to a place called Gethsemane, and He said to His disciples, "Sit here, while I go over there and pray." And taking with Him Peter and the two sons of Zebedee, He began to be sorrowful and troubled. Then He said to them, "My soul is very sorrowful, even to death; remain here, and watch with Me." And going a little farther He fell on His face and prayed, saying, "My Father, if it be possible, let this cup pass from Me; nevertheless, not as I will, but as You will." And He came to the disciples and found them sleeping. And He said to Peter, "So, could you not watch with Me one hour? Watch and pray that you may not enter into temptation. The spirit indeed is willing, but the flesh is weak." Again, for the second time, He went away and prayed, "My Father, if this cannot pass unless I drink it, Your will be done." And again, He came and found them sleeping, for their eyes were heavy. So, leaving them again, He went away and prayed for the third time, saying the same words again. Then He came to the disciples and said to them, "Sleep and take your rest later on. See, the hour is at hand, and the Son of Man is betrayed into the hands of sinners. Rise, let us be going; see, My betrayer is at hand."

Peter, in his arrogance, declares in verse 35, "Even if I must die with You, I will not deny You!" This statement shows clearly that he is overconfident in his ability to face difficulty and stress. His self-confidence is evident in his words, and yet in his actions his confidence fails him. On top of it all, Jesus declares in verse 34, "Truly, I tell you, this very night, before the rooster crows, you will deny Me three times." There is no greater humiliation than to make bold promises and predictions out of overconfidence and then fail miserably and completely.

Not only did Jesus articulate that Peter would deny Him but He also set the stage for his leadership failure along the way.

Many pastors in my experience fall prey to moments of brashness as pastoral leaders. It is very easy to be overcome with confidence when everyone within the parish defers to you and gives respect to the Office of the Holy Ministry. Satan can use that to cause you to believe that you, the one filling the office, are special. Remain vigilant and watchful to not be tempted to think that you are worthy or capable of yourself.

Thomas and Doubt

If you are at all normal in this life, you will have moments of doubt in your own ability and in what God seeks to do through you. Doubt can be overwhelming and, in some cases, completely crippling to the prospective leader. Throughout my pastoral career, I have had to work very hard to never let others see my doubt or see that their words or actions contributed to my doubt. But inevitably, I have had instances where my doubt shined through clearly to the people of God that I served.

One particular instance that showed my doubt was in 2007, when Our Savior Lutheran Church in Mount Lebanon, Pennsylvania, was in the merger process with Hope Lutheran Church in Upper Saint Clair, Pennsylvania. Though I had done a tremendous amount of work preparing for the merger meeting, I was worried that I had not done enough. I am certain that many of my members saw doubt in my eyes as I feared that God's will would be thwarted because of me. This was one of the most intense periods of doubt in my pastoral career.

It is not uncommon for believers—yes, even faithful pastors—to have these moments of doubt in both their personal lives and their lives of leadership. That is why the example of Thomas is so important for leaders to see the humanity of a faithful child of God. It can be quite easy for us to point the finger at Thomas as he was in disbelief at the resurrection of Jesus. Yet think back on your own moments of doubt as you consider his example in John 20:24–29:

> Now Thomas, one of the twelve, called the Twin, was not with them when Jesus came. So the other disciples told him, "We have seen the Lord." But he said to

> them, "Unless I see in His hands the mark of the nails, and place my finger into the mark of the nails, and place my hand into His side, I will never believe."
>
> Eight days later, His disciples were inside again, and Thomas was with them. Although the doors were locked, Jesus came and stood among them and said, "Peace be with you." Then He said to Thomas, "Put your finger here, and see My hands; and put out your hand and place it in My side. Do not disbelieve, but believe." Thomas answered Him, "My Lord and my God!" Jesus said to him, "Have you believed because you have seen Me? Blessed are those who have not seen and yet have believed."

The beauty in the story of Thomas in John's Gospel comes in these words of Jesus, "Have you believed because you have seen Me? Blessed are those who have not seen and yet have believed" (v. 29). Faithfulness to God is the totality of the Christian life. It is also an important factor during our moments of doubt and weakness. Faithfulness is that which the Holy Spirit provides us in Holy Baptism, and it strengthens in the moments of our lives where doubt creeps in and sometimes overcomes us. Being a faithful leader in God's kingdom centers around the complete trust that we have in Jesus Christ, our Lord and our Savior, regardless of the temptations that Satan lays before us.

Conclusion

As we have examined these Old and New Testament examples above, we can clearly see that some of the greatest leaders God has given throughout the Scriptures struggled at one point or another in their life of leadership. Whether you struggle with

- blaming others like Adam,
- feeling unqualified like Moses,
- hesitating like Gideon,
- experiencing guilt like David,
- being stubborn like Jonah,

- getting discouraged like Elijah,
- feeling unworthy like Isaiah,
- being brash like Peter, or
- feeling doubtful like Thomas,

God still rests on the faithful leaders that He has called and chosen to serve His Church and His people. Feelings of inadequacy in leadership should not be a deterrent to faithfully moving forward in joy and thanksgiving to serve the Lord and His Church. Take solace in the fact that these biblical leaders went on to be very important figures to God and the Church. Leading the people of God with integrity will come with feelings of inadequacy and moments of failure on the part of any sinful human person.

Key elements that should always be in play when dealing with the shortcomings of your pastoral leadership are reliance and trust that God will still work through you, with you, and by you according to His grace and mercy. The faithful servant of God should never doubt that the Lord has rested upon him and called him to serve in this way. Recognizing any one of these shortcomings in your life does not disqualify you from a faithful life of service to God in the Church.

REFLECTIONS

1. Which of these biblical leaders' inadequacies have you struggled with throughout your ministry and life?

2. How has this inadequacy caused difficulty in your ministry and leadership?

3. Identify biblical supports that remind you that God will still do great things in your life of leadership despite your inadequacy.

4. Discuss how, in each of these biblical leaders' lives, God overcame his inadequacy and used his strength to proclaim His love and mercy.

5. What are some of the techniques that you can utilize, from the biblical perspective, to fight against the temptations of Satan when looking in the mirror and seeing some of the difficulties previous leaders have struggled with?

CHAPTER II

Leading according to God's Plan

The biblical model of leadership begins with one simple command from Jesus: "You shall love the Lord your God with all your heart and with all your soul and with all your mind. . . . You shall love your neighbor as yourself" (Matthew 22:37, 39). This is the summary of all the laws that are given in the Bible. This is also the beginning of understanding what leading according to God's plan is all about. We are asked to love the Lord our God and love our neighbors as ourselves as a chief means of demonstrating the faith that lives in us by the power of the Holy Spirit. According to the Bible, loving the Lord our God and loving our neighbors is the key principle of the fulfillment of the Law.

Effective pastoral leaders understand that everything they do and say is generated out of deference, love, and respect for Christ. What that means is that effective pastoral leaders consistently approach difficult decision-making and problem-solving by answering the simple question "How does this glorify God and love our neighbor?" Too often throughout my years as a pastor, I have encountered fellow pastors who do not ask the question "How is my pastoral leadership loving God and loving my neighbor?" Too often, I have seen pastors who simply carry out their own will and exercise their strong hand in leadership to get their own way and flex their muscles as a leader. I am reminded of one instance where a pastor consistently demanded that the people of God in his congregation defer to him regardless of the circumstance.

Congregational ministry is divided into two distinct sections—the spiritual side and the corporation or business side. While these two distinct elements in the life of a congregation are clear, they also overlap. From the spiritual side, matters like worship, Bible instruction, visitation, and catechesis occur under the pastor's leadership. On the business side, distinct elements of operation and compliance occur. Some examples of the business side are governance and compliance with local, state, and federal law. While these two distinct elements of the life of a congregation are different, the pastor has connectivity and influence in both realms. Historically, many pastors have disassociated themselves from the business side and focused only on the spiritual side. It is my contention that issues on the business side of the church are often spiritual problems. This is why the pastor must be involved on both sides of the coin.

There is no doubt that pastoral leadership has a clear dividing line between spiritual and business things. The pastor's responsibility is 100 percent centered on the spiritual side, but it still has connective tissues on the business side. Effective pastoral leaders ought not to demand the same deference be given to them on the business side of the church as on the spiritual side. There is a distinct difference between these two realms within the life of the parish and the life of the pastoral leader.

Jesus sets the tone for pastoral leadership when, in John 15:13, He states, "Greater love has no one than this, that someone lay down his life for his friends." Effective pastoral leaders understand that loving their people and loving God are the core principles of leadership. Highly effective pastoral leaders are not motivated to love God and their neighbors by money, wealth, popularity, or even admiration. They are motivated by the amazing love God revealed to them through His Son, Jesus Christ. When leadership starts with focusing on loving God and loving their neighbors with Christ's sacrifice as the motivational underpinning, pastoral leaders will be successful and loved because they adhere to God's Word and follow Christ's command.

There cannot be any greater example of effective pastoral leadership than the example Jesus set in His life, ministry, sacrifice, death, and resurrection. The example that Jesus gives to all pastoral leaders is one that cannot be measured or duplicated. Loving without an expectation of a return or reward is what Jesus shows in the New Testament. Knowing that He will die for people who hate Him has always been a hallmark of Jesus' leadership style in the New Testament. Even those who loved and followed Jesus demonstrated a measure of distrust and fear at the hour that they were tested.

The apostle Peter is a perfect example of one of Jesus' trusted disciples who, when faced with his own leadership dilemma on the night when Jesus was betrayed, denied knowing Jesus three times. Even though Jesus predicted this at the Last Supper, Peter caved when the intense flame of social pressure descended on him that night. In fact, Peter, in fear, denied even knowing Jesus. His lack of love for Jesus and his lack of love for the other disciples became evident in fear as his own persecution and suffering came knocking at his doorstep. Peter, in this story, is a perfect example of what leadership should not be. He withered under the pressure of persecution and suffering. He did not measure the cost of loving God and loving his neighbor as Christ commands. His focus was solely on protecting himself and staving off personal persecution.

Too often, I see pastors who, out of fear for their ministry or of persecution, cower and shrink away from standing up to biblical principles and good pastoral leadership. Oftentimes, I have witnessed pastors who seek to protect their own selves and hold onto the respect and love of the people while rejecting the Word of God and not standing up for biblical principles. One example of this type of behavior is our pastors who refuse to preach against cohabitation out of fear that their members will become angry. There is no doubt that cohabitation has become a significant issue within the life of the church, and many within the church do not see it as a problem or sinful. This type of leadership is not effective or high quality in nature; it is simply cowardice and speaks of our sinful nature as human men serving in the Office of the Holy Ministry.

Jesus Did What He Asks Us to Do

One of the key biblical principles of effective pastoral leadership is to do the very things that you are asking others to do. If you as a pastoral leader are not willing to do those things you're asking your members to do, it will become obvious, and distrust will be created. When Jesus declared that "greater love has no one than this, that someone lay down his life for his friends" (John 15:13), He demonstrated this for the world in His suffering and death on the cross. Jesus went to the cross as an innocent victim and gave His life for sinful humanity. He showed by His own example that loving God and loving your neighbor is the starting point for all pastoral leadership decisions. Therefore, it becomes a much clearer vision for making leadership decisions.

All too often, I have witnessed pastoral leaders asking their laypeople to sacrifice time, talents, and treasures for the sake of the ministry while they themselves sacrifice little to nothing for the success of the ministry. It becomes apparent to congregational members when a pastor asks them to do things but he is not willing to do them himself. When I was a young boy, my parish pastor was very insistent on being an example to the people of God in the parish. That meant on a Sunday morning after getting six inches of snow from a severe winter storm, my pastor would be out shoveling the walkway to church long before other members were there. This had a lasting impression on me as it pertained to doing the very things that you ask your people to do. I understood that emulating my pastor was a good thing and something that showed love for God and love for my neighbor.

My own father was a quiet example of this leadership principle. He would not sit down and lecture me about the things I was supposed to do when it came to church and my life as a child of God. No, instead, he simply lived the baptismal life of loving God and loving his neighbor. For my siblings and me, church was not simply something that we did on Sundays and festivals. Instead, it was a lifestyle for us, and one that was normalized by my own father. My desire to be like my dad and my pastor was something that would bring honor to myself and my family. Being a leader meant simply doing the things necessary to support the church and its ministry.

As a new pastor out of the seminary, I met a local fellow Lutheran pastor who had been in his ministry for fifty-three consecutive years. One of the first things he told me was, "Your people will do as much as they see you doing in the parish." He would tell me stories of long ago when he first started in the parish and how he set the tone of ministry by leading by example. As a young pastor, I wondered about his example until I realized that my people would respond more positively to me when they saw me doing the very things I asked them to do. Over the course of my career, I have witnessed my people willing to go above and beyond because they trusted that I would do the same for them and for the sake of the ministry.

Following the example of Jesus, good pastoral leaders always do the very things they ask their laypeople to do when it comes to serving God and the church. Another example of this is financial stewardship within the congregational life. Faithful pastoral leaders understand that personal financial stewardship is a hallmark of any faithful Christian person. It is even more significant when it comes from the pastoral leader's position. Here again, laypeople can tell there is a disconnection when their pastoral leader is asking them to sacrifice in good stewardship to the church yet the pastor is not doing that himself. Hypocrisy is easily spotted, especially if it comes in the form of asking people to do things you, as a pastoral leader, are not willing to do yourself.

In my early years in the ministry, I was appointed to be a circuit visitor by the district president when the former circuit visitor took another call. I had a conflicted congregational situation in my circuit where several of the laity came to me with concerns about their pastor not contributing financially. It wasn't so much that they were judging how much he was giving, but rather the fact that he wasn't giving financially at all. They complained that he would preach and teach the importance of financial stewardship in the life of a Christian and then turn around and not contribute financially himself. When I confronted him on this matter, he was clear that his contribution to the church was his time. Let me be clear with the reader and say this: you must put your personal financial stewardship into practice to be an effective pastoral leader. If you don't, your laypeople will understand clearly that your teaching is centered around hypocrisy.

In my personal faith life, I can account for many examples where former pastors and adult leaders in my life provided me with high-quality examples of leadership. They set the tone and provided guidance on what leadership was supposed to look like in action. This helped shape me and mold me into the leader that I am today.

Too often, the satanic influence in our life causes us to encourage others to do the right thing while we ourselves steer clear of the God-pleasing behaviors called for in the Scriptures. This is especially true with pastors who can be tempted to proclaim the Law of God clearly and not let it apply to themselves. Effective pastoral leaders understand that everything they proclaim, declare, and teach describes the life of a Christian and must also apply to themselves as well.

Personal Devotional Life

Another key component to effective pastoral leadership is living by the example of Jesus Himself in your personal devotional life. An effective pastoral leader cannot teach his people that they must have a personal prayer life and a scriptural study life if he is not engaging in the same things personally. Often in the ministry of Jesus, He would go away to pray and converse with His Father. In fact, on Maundy Thursday, Jesus spent a great deal of time praying to His Father. Upon returning to His disciples, He chastised them for falling asleep while He was praying. Likewise, on the Mount of Transfiguration, Jesus went to pray, taking with Him Peter, James, and John as Moses and Elijah came and stood among them as they talked. In these cases, Jesus was making it clear that His prayer life was important and a significant part of what He did as a child of the heavenly Father.

Effective pastoral leaders fully understand that having a devout prayer life and a dedicated scriptural study life is a key component to maintaining spiritual health and wellness. However, when a pastoral leader teaches his people to do this and then decides that it's not important for him, it becomes obvious that he is a hypocrite. In fact, in my experience, pastors who do not have a prayer life and a biblical study life are found out by the very people they're teaching. During my ministry, I have had very educated laymen and women who have held my feet to the fire of knowing the Word of God and living by it. It has always been a tremendous blessing and a great joy to serve these laypeople. I have had the pleasure of being partners in ministry rather than adversaries.

While being a vicar in Brookings, South Dakota, I had a blessed woman who said to me one night at a Lenten supper, "Vicar, if you're going to tell a member you're going to pray for them, make sure you do it." At the time, I was perplexed as to why she felt the need to tell me that. Later that evening, I got up the courage to ask her why she had said that, and she told me a story of a pastor in her history who told her that he would pray for a specific situation in her life. Later, when she went to give him an update, he did not know what she was talking about and admitted to not praying for her. The damage was clear on the woman's face, and I learned a significant pastoral leadership lesson that night. Do what you say you will do for your people.

Effective pastoral leaders understand that they can be encouraging and inspiring to people if they're willing to do the very things that they ask their people to do themselves. Jesus provides us with great examples of Him not only following through with what He promises but also asking us to do likewise. To love God and love your neighbor as a pastoral leader, you must be committed to doing the very things you ask others to do. You must also be willing to do the necessary things for a given situation, understanding that no one may see you doing it and you may not get credit for it from anyone.

Business Planning for Judging

Over my lifetime as a pastor, many people have argued with me about whether the Bible speaks directly to the topic of leadership. In fact, I have had people tell me that the Bible has no leadership examples within it. Early on in my ministry, I would have agreed with the principle that the Bible does not speak authoritatively on the topic of leadership. It was not until I began my studies in my doctoral program that it was presented to me that biblical leadership and structured business planning are laid out at the very outset of the Old Testament. In the Book of Exodus, for example, we see a clear model of the world's first business plan and leadership structure.

Moses' father-in-law, Jethro, laid out for Moses in Exodus 18 a clear leadership plan and principles that articulated how Moses should judge different matters within the Israelite community. Jethro inquired of Moses, saying, "What is this that you are doing for [these] people? Why do you sit alone, and all the people stand around you from morning till evening?" (v. 14). Moses had gotten into a habit of judging every single problem that occurred within the life of the Israelites. As the biblical text reminds us, Moses would sit from morning until evening listening to disputes and judging them. Jethro was keenly aware that Moses would do nothing but run himself ragged if he maintained this pace of judging disputes. So Jethro laid out for Moses a judging system that would lighten his burden. Jethro told Moses to seek men from among the people who fear God, hate bribes, and are trustworthy. He then instructed Moses to establish multiple tiers that these men would judge. This would allow only the most serious matters to be brought before Moses to judge.

Jethro knew that this would make life much easier for Moses as he carried out his responsibilities among the people of Israel. While this might seem logical after reading the Exodus text, I would venture to say that in most cases, pastoral leaders do not do a good enough job of delegating responsibilities to others. Much like Moses in this biblical story, most pastoral leaders believe they must do everything themselves and not relinquish anything that is their responsibility. Effective pastoral leaders learn how and when to delegate responsibilities and tasks. The pastoral leader who refuses to delegate and give up responsibilities generally becomes burned out and emotionally, as well as mentally, exhausted.

This is a very difficult principle for hardworking pastoral leaders to grasp. You don't need to do everything within the ministry yourself. Leading from the pastoral office means you trust other people to accomplish tasks, but they can accomplish them with your input, advice, and guidance. I have seen too many faithful, hardworking, and dedicated pastoral leaders burn themselves out trying to bear the entire weight of the ministry on their shoulders. One of the wisest pastors I've had in my life reminded me that the greatest pastors understand their own limitations and know how to delegate responsibilities in ministry. This shows that you shouldn't be like Moses in the Exodus story, believing that you alone must bear the entire burden of the work of the ministry yourself. Listen to the advice that Moses' father-in-law, Jethro, gave him, "Moreover, look for able men from all the people, men who fear God, who are trustworthy and hate a bribe" (v. 21) and empower them to do things within the ministry so that you can focus on those things that are the most needed.

This principle of leadership transcends all areas, businesses, and responsibilities. Delegation as a leader is a discerning task that all effective leaders must at some point or another learn to master. Delegating responsibility also denotes partnership and collaboration in matters of ministry in congregational life. I have often witnessed situations where pastors were unwilling to delegate and partner with their laypeople to be effective and efficient in ministry and mission for the sake of Christ in the church. In almost every case, I have seen conflict and ministry failure occurring because of selfish leadership pride. Do not allow Satan to infect you with this pride and cause you to believe that you are the only one who can accomplish the task. Partnering in ministry means trusting one another, which comes in the form of having faith in one another and fulfilling the command of Christ to love your neighbor.

The example that Jesus sets time and time again in the Scriptures is based on trust and love. He instructs His disciples to do various tasks and chores, and they accomplish them, even those tasks and chores that at first seem ridiculous. When Jesus called Peter, James, and John, the biblical text reminds us that they were cleaning their nets after a failed night's fishing. Ironically, Jesus asks them to set out into deep water to let down their nets to go fishing. While they were frustrated and even potentially upset, they did as He asked out of deference and love. What was returned to them for their faithfulness in trusting Jesus was a boat so full of fish that it almost sank (see Luke 5:1–11). Trust in what God says He will do with, through, and by you. Trust the relationships and people God has placed into your life that will allow you to accomplish far more in partnership than you could accomplish by yourself.

Christ Finished the Task

One of the greatest examples of leadership we have in the entire Bible is the Son of God, Jesus, doing the will of His Father. At almost every turn in the biblical story, Jesus faced reasons and trials that should have given Him cause to say, "No, I will not continue." From His temptation in the wilderness, where He hungered and thirsted, to His beating and whipping before His crucifixion, Jesus had reasons that any one of us could have used to simply say, "I quit." From the beginning of humanity until this very day, Satan has preyed on our weak flesh and our soft spirit. Trials and temptations are reasons we might simply say, "No more." Effective pastoral leaders understand that saying "No more" when things get tough is not an option.

Recently, I was talking to a fellow pastor in my district who was telling me of some strife and misery within his congregation. He described a recent meeting where people of his congregation were piling accusations on him and his wife for certain failures within the ministry. He told me in detail how it was hurtful and burdensome to listen to the mean and angry words that were being used to inform him how bad he was as a leader. He continued to tell me that as he was sitting at the meeting and listening to these things, the thought ran through his mind that he did not deserve all this abuse and that he could retire now and not look back. This is what Satan wants all pastoral leaders to feel when things get tough and the misery of leadership sets in.

Simply put, quitting or stopping is not an option for effective pastoral leaders. Throwing in the towel cannot be the go-to move when things get difficult and painful. While it may be the most appealing and, in some cases, the most logical, you cannot allow yourself to default to this as a means of escape. Jesus understood this clearly and pointedly. And yet, on Maundy Thursday, there in the Garden of Gethsemane, Jesus pleaded with His Father to remove this cup of suffering from Him. He asked earnestly for the Father to find another way for salvation and forgiveness to be accomplished so that the immense pain and suffering would not need to take place. Jesus was fortified in spirit by the Holy Ghost, and He remained resolute to fulfill His Father's will. Let the affliction and pain of such moments in your ministry drive you to your knees to pray to the Father and your Lord Jesus so the Spirit can fortify you too.

Effective pastoral leaders understand that finishing the task given to them is something that ranks very high on the priority list of leadership. Not succumbing to pressure and pain, hurt and anguish is a mark of good leadership. Standing your ground, knowing that the Lord will not forsake you at the very hour of your need, is a hallmark of Christian faith and life. Remembering the great command of Christ to love God and love your neighbor in the role of pastoral leader is what sets you apart from everyone else within the church.

Jesus cried from the cross after being forsaken in our place. He faced loneliness for us so that we will never be forsaken by the Father in heaven. Jesus went to the very depths of hell to free those captives there. He provides us with a clear picture of how loving God and loving our neighbor point us toward leading in a God-pleasing manner. His deep trust and faith provide a clear and concise example for all who serve in faith and love toward our God.

Conclusion

Leadership is commanded by God. His plan for everyone in leadership is for them to love God and love their neighbor as a central principle of pastoral leadership. There is no doubt that effective pastoral leaders understand this principle clearly and carry it out as effectively as possible. Measuring everything against loving God and loving his neighbor allows the pastoral leader to keep the focus where it belongs—on Christ and the message of forgiveness. By holding forth a specific understanding of loving God and loving their neighbor, pastoral leaders can see the life of Christ in action within their ministry.

We see Jesus doing the very things that He asks us to do, namely, giving your life for your friend. Jesus hung upon the cross in love for His fallen creation, knowing that in all cases His innocence was payment for their guilt. Still, Jesus went forth following the commands of His Father that had been set forth after the fall into sin. Time and again, He could have come up with excuses and reasons for not continuing or finishing the salvific works of His Father. And yet, He went forth in love. He finished the task and accomplished the goal of salvation and forgiveness.

Discipline in the life of a pastoral leader is important as well. Setting aside time for personal spiritual growth and scriptural renewal by way of prayer is a key principle for effective pastoral leaders. Having a personal devotional and scriptural study life is a component that most successful pastors understand and practice daily. Demonstrating to your people that your own personal devotional life is important is a fantastic means of leading by example. Setting the tone of loving your neighbor by praying for them is one way that an effective pastoral leader can be successful.

Order and structure in the life of a pastor become very important toward success in the ministry. Having a plan and the ability to delegate to accomplish that plan is a hallmark of any good pastoral leader. Jethro, the father-in-law of Moses, understood this clearly in the Old Testament story of the judging system of Israel. Jethro realized that Moses needed to engage in a system that would not drive him to exhaustion. He established the levels of judging to demonstrate partnership in the ministry and effective management of situations. To be an effective pastoral leader is to understand that delegation and partnership in the Gospel. This is extremely important for the success of the ministry and the longevity of the pastor. Maintaining a healthy physical balance in life assists in longevity and productivity.

Complete the tasks that are before you in leadership and do not leave things unfinished because they are difficult. Do not leave tasks undone or situations ignored for the sake of ease or simplicity. Effective pastoral leaders will complete the tasks set before them and reconcile all those unreconciled situations. For the effective pastoral leader, the difficulty never becomes an excuse nor means to declare, "No more." Don't allow Satan to convince you that the pastoral task ahead of you is difficult, so therefore you simply shouldn't do it. Some of the hardest tasks in ministry are some of the most rewarding things you will endure in your career. Loving members enough to discipline them in hopes of repentance, contrition, and forgiveness is the hallmark of the office of high-quality and effective pastoral leadership.

REFLECTIONS

1. What kind of leader are you? What kind of leader do you want to be?

2. Do you do the tasks and work that you ask the people of God to do?

3. List some tasks that you believe are just lay member tasks and some that are pastoral tasks.

4. What are the benefits of leading by example?

5. Do you have a plan for what ministry you will do and how you will carry that plan out?

6. Think of the goals you had when you first began ministry in your parish. How many of these goals have you had a chance to accomplish? Which ones are still outstanding and in need of attention?

7. List the goals for your next two years in the parish.

8. Do you have a problem delegating work to others in the church?

9. What are some of the ways you can engage more members in the leadership roles that are needed within the congregation?

CHAPTER III

Difficulties as a Pastoral Leader

There is no doubt about it, being a pastoral leader is a difficult and stressful endeavor. The calling from our heavenly Father to lead His people can be painful at times and emotionally difficult. The simple point is that being a pastoral leader means there will come times when people will not like what you have to say and will likely not be happy with what you do. Nonetheless, you must understand that the wolves will still come for the sheep, and the shepherd still must stand his ground without fear or timidity as he cares for the sheep of Christ.

In all stressful situations, there are clearly two potential responses that occur. You either stand and fight back against the difficulty before you, or you flee and run away as a means of self-preservation. These opposing responses are natural, and all leaders face them in times of stress and difficulty. Pastoral leaders will face these moments far more than most other leaders will. This is due in large part to the need for a pastoral leader to clearly defend the Word of God.

Regardless of the leadership challenges and difficulties that pastoral leaders will face as shepherds of the flock, pastoral leaders must remain resolute and steadfast in the callings in which God has placed them. Those called into the pastoral leadership role are as human as the sheep they serve. What this means is that Satan will come for them much harder. For if Satan can remove the shepherd from the sheep, the sheep themselves will wander aimlessly and forever seek direction and protection. While it is true that the shepherds of the flock are as sinful as the sheep they serve, the shepherds also must consistently strive to live a godly life.

When I became a district president in 2015, I was amazed at the number of pastoral leaders who struggled in their personal life or their family life. I wasn't naive to the fact that fellow clergymen had some difficulties or problems; I simply was amazed at how many brother clergymen had so many significant things going on in their lives. Satan was trying to distract them from their work at hand and turn their eyes away from the forgiving message of salvation and mercy. It was not until my first disciplinary action as a district president that I understood the immense pressure that Satan places on the pastoral leader within a congregation.

Too often, the laity of a congregation elevates the pastoral leader to a place he does not deserve as a fellow sinful child of God. Therefore, when a pastor struggles personally, professionally, or within his own family, it is very difficult for the laity to understand why. Because of this pressure, I have seen many situations where pastors have caused themselves far greater difficulties in pastoral leadership by what they did or did not do as it related to themselves or their families. Being a pastoral leader brings along its own set of difficulties. Having personal or family difficulties only adds to the stress and pressure of being in the pastoral office.

While I was a student at the seminary, it was emphasized to me on many occasions that the order of importance in the life of a pastor or a seminary student was God, family, and the church. But I have had problems with that order at times in my ministry. The church has, at times in my ministry, jostled ahead of my family due to a compulsion to be an effective pastoral leader. Anyone who has served in the Office of the Ministry knows that when the call comes from the hospital late at night or early in the morning and the voice on the other end tells you that one of their family members is near death, your first reaction is to go. I remember when my middle son, Nathaniel, was a baby. I was putting him to bed when the phone rang and I was told that one of my members had taken a turn for the worse and the family was being told he did not have long to live. I distinctly remember handing my son to my wife, changing my clothes like Superman in a phone booth, and tearing off for the hospital to be with the family. At that moment, church became more important than my family. As difficult as it was for the church to supersede my family at that moment, to be an effective pastoral leader, I needed to go.

When new seminarians are assigned to congregations in my district, I have a very clear speech that I give them pertaining to the difficulties that they will face as pastoral leaders. Tough times will come. Satan will bring temptation, pain, and suffering, but I remind seminarians that the Lord shall not leave nor forsake them. I am reminded of the Old Testament story of Joseph, as his father and brothers come to Egypt during the famine so that he can provide them with food. When his brothers fear Joseph will repay them for selling him into slavery, the beautiful text of the Genesis account reminds us of this significant point: "As for you, you meant evil against me, but God meant it for good, to bring it about that many people should be kept alive, as they are today" (Genesis 50:20). This beautiful reminder to any pastoral leader is that even when our fellow believers mean harm and pain to us, God can make it serve His good purposes.

Being an effective pastoral leader means understanding that God can use difficulties for good. In fact, I have seen some of the best pastoral care given by brothers in the ministry while they were under the greatest persecution and suffering difficulty in their parish. When their eyes are forced on Christ and His Word and no longer on themselves, pastoral leaders tend to reduce their work to the simplest common denominator—the Word of God and His promises. Much like in the Old Testament story of Joseph, where his brothers sold him into slavery, pastoral leaders have events in the life of their church and ministry that can be catastrophic and life-changing. And yet, as was the case with Joseph, God can use it for His good purposes and for the glorification of the Gospel.

Effective pastoral leaders understand that tough times will not remain forever. That difficulty in ministry is short-lived when our eyes are on the cross of Christ. Even in those cases where we as pastoral leaders are the cause of the difficulties we are experiencing, God can show mercy and bring good from those very difficulties.

Focus on Who Is in Charge

Most pastoral leaders from time to time can lose focus on who is in charge and why they are experiencing difficulties and problems. Congregational conflict and stress within a given context can easily force pastoral leaders away from their focus, and they may start to forget who is in charge. Creating conflict and strife is just one technique that Satan uses to pull our eyes away from God's plan and His purpose. Pastoral leaders must remember that it is not our work and ourselves that matter. Rather, it is what God can and will do through us, by us, and despite us. This reality is a key component for any successful pastoral leader.

I can recall a moment early on in my ministry when I was forced to stop relying on myself and start relying on God. I remember day after day walking into the sanctuary at church, kneeling before the altar, and asking God to simply see it my way. In the midst of this difficult situation in my early pastoral life, I was more focused on what was happening and the difficulty it was bringing me rather than on what God was doing through it. As in anything else in life, looking back retrospectively on the situation, I see how and what God was doing for the sake of the Gospel and in my pastoral leadership life. However, as a sinful human person, I was not focused on what God was doing but rather on the part that I was playing. This taught me a significant life lesson that has not left me to this very day. Remembering who is in charge of the life of a congregation is key to being an effective pastoral leader.

Years ago, I would often go on home visits to one of my members with whom I was very close in the congregation. From time to time, I would complain and moan about conditions in the parish and relationships with certain members. I distinctly remember the day that my member reminded me that I was not in control nor was I dictating the outcome. While the initial hearing of this from my member caused frustration and anger, I quickly settled down and thought about what he said. He was right—I was spending too much time thinking about my own desired outcome and how to achieve it rather than allowing God's will to be done in the church.

It is very easy for pastoral leaders to lose focus on who is in charge and why we do the work that we do. Time and time again throughout the biblical narrative, we see great biblical figures losing focus and fulfilling their desires rather than the plan that God had put before them. Whether we think about Abraham, Jacob, Noah, or any of the Old Testament figures, they all seemed to go wrong when they forgot who was in charge and for what purpose they were carrying out their leadership roles.

Making Tough Choices in Ministry

No matter what type of leadership position we are discussing, making tough choices is simply the role of a leader. Pastoral leaders must make tough choices in ministry that likely will not be popular. Nevertheless, being a pastoral leader means that at times you will be unpopular in making certain decisions and choices. Whether you're deciding to admit a guest to the Lord's Supper or deciding to invoke the minor ban, inevitably you will have tough choices to make. Unfortunately, in my time as a district president, I have seen way too many pastoral leaders take the cowardly approach and not make tough decisions that they think will be unpopular. Tough decisions come with being a pastoral leader. Don't be afraid of making tough choices in your ministry.

Early on in my career, I realized that there were only two avenues I could travel. I could either let difficulty pass by and not address the situation or I could address the difficult situation and likely offend and anger certain members of the congregation. I remember talking to a veteran pastor in the area about a difficult situation that I had to deal with, and he simply said to me, "Don't be afraid to do what is best for the ministry and right in the eyes of God." He then followed it up by reminding me that you will always have unhappy people and dissatisfied members when you do what's right in the eyes of God. Nonetheless, he made it clear to me (and this point has never left me): you must not be afraid to do what is best for the ministry. Do not be afraid to make difficult choices.

My advice to young pastors these days is very clear when dealing with tough choices. I remind them not to be afraid of the hard decisions in ministry; God will guide them and give them clarity on what to do, especially when it's being done in His name. This is the prayer of the Church, that the Holy Spirit would guide and lead us in all that we do and say to glorify God. The Bible never promises pastoral leaders that ministry will be easy; however, it does promise that the Lord will not leave us or forsake us at the very hour of our need. The wisdom that is required to make difficult choices is being given by the power of the Holy Spirit to those who serve in the office. As pastoral leaders within God's Church, we ought always to focus on the truth that He will provide us with what we need at the hour that we need it.

It is clear to me after two-plus decades of serving God in the church that hard decisions take courage and strength. That courage and that strength come from faith in the promise that God will be with you in everything you do in His name. Focusing on the truth of the Scriptures in pastoral leadership will always bring comfort and strength when difficult decisions need to be made. This point is clearly driven home in Jesus' exhortation in the twelfth chapter of John's Gospel, where He states, "For I have not spoken on My own authority, but the Father who sent Me has Himself given Me a commandment—what to say and what to speak. And I know that His commandment is eternal life. What I say, therefore, I say as the Father has told Me" (John 12:49–50). Effective pastoral leaders must understand that the same exact point applies to them. The Father has told us in His Word, and we must believe, teach, and confess it ourselves as pastoral leaders within His Church.

There is no doubt that Satan will use fear to keep you from making good choices in ministry and leading in a God-pleasing manner. Our faith in the power of God and in the gift of the Holy Spirit allows us to focus on what the Father has told us in the Scriptures and what He has asked of us in pastoral leadership in the congregations with which He has blessed us. Fear cannot be the dominating factor in the tough choices you make in ministry. Difficult ministry decisions must be made with trust and faith that God will provide all that you need to make an effective and God-pleasing decision. Likewise, we must believe in the words of Romans 8:28, "And we know that for those who love God all things work together for good, for those who are called according to His purpose."

It Is Lonely at the Top

When you are the leader of any business, ministry, church, or endeavor, the old adage is absolutely true: it is lonely at the top. While there is no hard evidence that can prove this proverb, those who are in significant leadership positions or in the Office of the Holy Ministry can attest to this reality. Perhaps even more than being *lonely* at the top, it is *isolating* to be the leader of a ministry or church. Loneliness and isolation produce the same difficulties for pastoral leaders. The loneliness comes from being the one responsible and yet not the one always making all the decisions. Being the one who must stand up against the onslaught of the devil and protect the sheep of God in and of itself creates loneliness.

When I was elected bishop and president of the English District in 2015, life for me changed radically that day. Brothers whom I had been friends with for years changed the way that they talked to me and treated me. It was as if in some way, after being elected bishop, I became a different person. This is an example of how being at the top can create loneliness. Being the leader of a congregation or an organization carries with it significant pressures and stressors (whether real or perceived) that can only be understood or felt when you sit in that top position.

It is very clear to me that many people desire to be in the top position of leadership within a congregation or a ministry. This reality quickly changes when difficult decisions need to be made and the criticisms of your decision-making get louder and louder. In some respects, I fell prey to this when I was a vice president under Bishop David Stechholz. It seemed easy to be the bishop from my perspective as vice president—until I became bishop myself and realized the pressures and criticisms were much more intense once I sat in the seat of leadership. It is impossible to describe to those desiring to be at the top of an organization or a ministry what the stressors and pressures are like. It is even more difficult to prepare somebody for the extreme criticisms and naysaying he will face when making decisions from the position of leadership.

One reality that I did not understand until I became a leader in the church was the extreme frequency of those who second-guessed the decisions I made and asked why I made them. This in and of itself can also create loneliness and isolation when you are the leader of an organization or a church. In many respects, when you are not the leader of the organization, you likewise do not have all the facts necessary to make the decisions within the organization. This can lead to criticism and second-guessing of your decision-making because full facts and information are not present to those outside of the leadership circle.

As an effective pastoral leader, you must understand that loneliness and isolation at the top are simply a reality of fulfilling the office. The biblical adage is true: "Many are called, but few are chosen" (Matthew 22:14). Those who are chosen also bear the responsibility of carrying out the will of God in that place. This is not the reality for those who are not in leadership. They can criticize and second-guess the decisions and positions of the leader without the ramifications of being responsible. This is a key reason why it is lonely at the top as a pastoral leader. It's very easy for people to get angry with the pastor when he refuses to commune them because they're living in open adultery. The burden of proclaiming the Gospel is that Satan tries to convince our members that their sins are not anywhere as grievous as their neighbor's; therefore, they ought to be free to do anything they want that satisfies their hearts and minds.

However, do not be deterred by the loneliness and isolation that come from being an effective pastoral leader. We seek to do the will of God as leaders in His Church without fear or trepidation. Effective pastoral leaders make decisions that glorify God and proclaim Jesus to the world rather than seek popularity and acclaim. It is lonely at the top as a leader because the burdens that are borne by the office are not for everyone to share. The effective pastoral leader understands this reality and is not intimidated by it. Know this: there will be many who desire to be in the leadership position whom God has not chosen.

As a pastoral leader, you must remember that God will accomplish His will through you despite your frailty, failings, and sinful life. God is merciful, and He has a plan for your service in His kingdom. Despite our own sinfulness and selfish desires, He will accomplish all that He wants according to His will and His way. Trust that the Lord will do His work through you and despite you.

You Are Not Always Going to Be Right

One of the difficult realities in the life of any young pastoral leader is coming to grips with the fact that he will not always be right about everything. This is hard, especially for men, to understand, and it is even more difficult for pastors to understand. When you deal with concrete reality—namely, the Scriptures—where truth and absolute authority are given, Satan can confuse you into believing that you are always right, regardless of the circumstances. Difficulty within a congregational ministry can occur when the pastoral leader refuses to accept that he is not right in each situation.

During my vicarage year, I learned a significant life lesson about not always being right in ministry. The congregation I was serving was going through a building phase in addition to their ministry. At a key juncture in the building project, a significant decision needed to be made about the color of the carpet. I remember sitting at the voters meeting where this was discussed and watching people passionately defend their position. More important, I remember that my vicarage supervisor leaned over to me and reminded me that certain things within the church are not worthy of believing that you are right about. There is no theological significance to the color of the carpet in any congregation.

Personal preference and theological integrity are two different things. The effective pastoral leader understands that his influence and calling by God is to defend the biblical fidelity and confessional integrity of any congregation or individual. Understanding clearly as a pastoral leader that you will not always be right about matters of opinion is a key factor in being successful in pastoral ministry. A wise pastor once told me that there are certain church decisions that a pastor should never get involved in or use pastoral capital to complete.

On the other hand, when you are wrong or when you have said something wrong, the simple point is this: you should take responsibility for what you've said or done. Accepting responsibility is very difficult for anyone, let alone those who serve in a public office that is visible and authoritative. Accepting responsibility publicly for things you've said or done that are inappropriate or wrong is not only the appropriate action for a pastoral leader but also simply wise to do. When an apology is needed, simply apologize publicly. Too often in the life of pastors, it is much easier to not take responsibility as the leader. Rather, we may be tempted to sit back and simply take the passive approach in leadership by allowing things to go haywire and then pointing the finger at others to dispel blame and responsibility. This is a selfish, sinful human trait that prevents us from being vulnerable to our own sin.

Admitting a mistake publicly is critically important. It is also important that you do not remain too critical of yourself. The reality is others will do that for you very readily and quickly, especially when your transgression is done in public. I have found that in my life as a pastor whenever I have misspoken or done something in a public fashion, it is easily remedied with a public apology and accountability. When a sin is committed in public, contrition and repentance must also occur in public. Effective pastoral leaders understand this and practice it regularly in their ministry. When pastoral leaders understand that they will not always be right, their life as a pastoral leader becomes somewhat easier, understanding that love covers a multitude of sins.

As a district president, I have the pleasure of doing the installations for new pastors at congregations across my district. One of the greatest moments that I enjoy during an installation service is the congregation promising that they will put the best construction on everything when it comes to the life of their pastor. In that installation liturgy, I am always struck by the phraseology that "love covers a multitude of sins" (1 Peter 4:8). When public confession is done by the pastor, public absolution is given by God's people. This is a beautiful reality that we, God's children, enjoy as forgiven sinners.

Conclusion

The simple reality is you will have various difficulties at points in your ministry as a pastoral leader. This is natural and normal during a leader's life. This reality should not dissuade men from considering becoming pastoral leaders. It is a reality that exists for anyone in leadership positions. Whether you lead in a congregation, a corporation, or a business setting, difficulties are a part of being a leader. One important difference, however, in serving within the church is that we believe and trust that God's will will be done indeed within the life of the congregation administration.

You must keep a clear focus on who is in charge when it comes to effective pastoral leadership. Losing focus on who is in charge and why you are doing what you're doing will only lead to conflict within the ministry. Never fall prey to the idea that you are on your own as a pastoral leader. God is with you, and He will provide all that you need to support your leadership decisions and outcomes in the ministry.

Don't be afraid to make tough choices in ministry. Being an effective pastoral leader means that tough choices will need to be made regardless of where you are and who you are. God has set apart the pastoral office to make tough choices within the ministry context. Do not allow Satan to cause you to be afraid of making those decisions. Be bold and have confidence that God will guide you and lead you.

Loneliness and isolation are a reality of the leadership position. Do not shy away from this reality as a pastoral leader. It is natural for individuals outside of the leadership position to question and argue about the decisions that you make. Find other leaders you can trust and talk to them about the challenges that you face in pastoral leadership. One of the greatest blessings that I have as a district president is attending the council of presidents' meetings four times a year. It is at these meetings that I can share the frustrations, joys, and struggles of being a district president in The Lutheran Church—Missouri Synod. It will be lonely on top, so seek a brother in Christ who can alleviate the loneliness and the isolation as a father, confessor, or confidant.

While difficulty within the pastoral office will inevitably occur, our faith and trust are in Christ alone. We believe in the promise of God that He shall not leave nor forsake His people. Time and time again throughout the Scriptures, we see instances where hope seemed lost and where God delivered. In many cases in the biblical story of Moses and the children of Israel, God promised Moses that He would go before him to accomplish the tasks that He was setting Moses and the children of Israel out to do. Have faith and trust in every difficult situation that God has already gone before you and that He will strengthen you in your time of need. It is by the grace of God alone that we have success, and it is by the grace of God alone that we are fruitful in His name for the sake of the Gospel.

REFLECTIONS

1. What are some of the issues that you are now having in leadership that you did not expect before you became a pastor?

2. What guides you in your ministry and life as a leader? List some ways you track how you lead and what is motivating you.

3. It is very easy to isolate and become a lone ranger. How can you stay connected and be associated with a support system that will aid you in your work and leadership?

4. Who are your confessors and mentors? How often do you speak to them and rely on them for advice and help?

5. Journal your experiences and evaluate your mistakes in order to keep from making those same mistakes again in the future.

CHAPTER IV

Leading, Not Following

As a college student, I was told that there are two types of leaders. Some lead from out front, and some follow and remain in the background. For me, there is no doubt about it: God is calling pastoral leaders to lead from the front rather than from behind. Throughout the biblical narrative, we see time and time again that God has an ultimate purpose and plan for those who serve in the Office of the Public Ministry. From Noah to Abraham, Joseph to Moses, and throughout the entirety of the New Testament, God sets apart His leaders for clear and definite reasons.

I acknowledge that God has provided each one of us with different skills that allow us to be effective in various leadership roles within the church. I also acknowledge that God calls us to lead with integrity and with biblical fidelity. What that means is that being a leader requires courage and the ability to understand that people will not always appreciate what you do. They will have criticisms and complaints about your choices and your positions. Oftentimes, they will likely not even have the whole story or all the facts but will still feel the need to complain and criticize.

The simple reality that God has placed you in a leadership role within the church as a pastor should provoke in you an understanding of God's purpose in your life. All of us in the Office of the Holy Ministry are called for a purpose. That purpose is to lead God's people forth in faith and trust, and move toward our neighbor as Christ commanded. Too often, however, I have witnessed pastors take a back seat to the will of lay leadership out of fear that those members would leave the congregation.

Upon my installation at Our Savior Lutheran Church in Mount Lebanon, Pennsylvania, the president of the congregation asked me if I was going to become a Pittsburgh Steelers fan. My reply, which set the tone for my ministry at the church, was clearly, "No." As a lifelong Detroit Lions fan, I was not going to replace my allegiance to the Lions with the Steelers. However, the definitive nature of my answer gave the people of God a clear understanding of the type of leader that I was. Peer pressure and public scrutiny were not going to cause me to waffle or shift from the position that I had. I know this example is somewhat weak, in that a vast majority of this scenario was lighthearted joking. Nonetheless, the leadership approach that I have brought since day one to the pastoral office is definitive and true.

Early on in my ministry, I witnessed a new pastor in a neighboring congregation quickly fold to the pressures of the lay leadership within his congregation. He took the pastoral approach that his laymen and women were leading the congregation and his role was to simply preach on Sundays and teach Bible class. While I wholeheartedly ascribe to those two functions being highly important in the life of the pastor, I argued with him at the time that he still bore the responsibility of leading the people of God rather than following the lead of his laymen and women. Over the next decade, he struggled mightily as a pastor in his congregation in large part because the church had a pastor who lacked leadership and was afraid of criticism and pressure.

Leadership of Fear

Over the course of my career, I have witnessed many pastoral leaders make decisions within the ministry that were pressured by overbearing laymen and women who threatened to withdraw their contribution or leave the congregation if they did not get their way. In scenario after scenario, I witnessed pastors relinquish their God-given responsibility to lead the congregation only to appease an angry layman who wanted a specific decision made and was not willing to accept any other decision. Anytime pastoral leaders make decisions based on threats of a member leaving or transferring, they have followed rather than led.

I acknowledge that in many cases fear drives a pastor to follow rather than lead. Fear can be an overwhelming weight for a pastoral leader who puts his faith in sinful humans and not in God. Early on in my career, my congregation was not that large at all. We had between sixty and seventy-five people worshiping on a Sunday, and any one strategic family leaving the church could have put the ministry in great jeopardy or peril. I understand fully how the threat of the laymen leaving the congregation or withholding their offering unless they get their way can cause pastoral leaders to act in fear rather than in faith.

As a district president, I have had countless conversations with pastors who have called me and asked my advice on how to deal with this situation or that situation based on the threat of a layperson withholding their offering or leaving the congregation. My advice in every one of these scenarios always ends the same way. I ask the pastor a simple question: "Do you trust in God or in man?" Never in the seminary training that pastoral leaders receive nor in the school of hard knocks is it promised that being a leader is going to be easy or fun. I have had many moments within my ministry when fear gripped my spirit and could have controlled my leadership style and decision-making.

Fear in life is normal and natural. Strong pastoral leaders understand that fear cannot be eliminated but must be controlled. Recently, I was watching a television show about phobias and fears and how to overcome them. Throughout the entirety of the television special, it was made clear that facing your fears is the only way to overcome them. As a pastoral leader, Christ faced the fear of forsakenness from His Father in our place. For any faithful child of God who has been called to the office of a pastor, fear cannot overcome you.

The promises of God are sure and true for us to this day. Jesus promises that He shall never leave or forsake His people at their very greatest hour of need. This promise from God is one that was demonstrated time and time again in the Old Testament from the great biblical stories of Abraham, Isaac, and Jacob to the accounts of Moses and David. The power of God and His mighty hand is clear and evident. When hope seemed lost and victory swiped from God's people, His might and power shown forth and came through.

Having a Purpose in Leadership

Motivation and purpose are both key traits of effective pastoral leaders. Mark 10:45 states, "For even the Son of Man came not to be served but to serve, and to give His life as a ransom for many." Jesus had a purpose in life; His purpose was to serve and seek the lost. His motivation was love, and He desired that all His creation would be saved. The clear purpose of Jesus Christ was to save the world and to restore it to a right relationship with the Father. This motivation continues today in the Office of the Pastoral Ministry. All men who serve in the pastoral office understand the message of the Gospel and the motivation of the Gospel. This Gospel motivation is what drives pastoral leaders and sustains the work of the office.

Because God has given us different gifts and different abilities, it is critically important that all who are in the role of leader within the pastoral office understand that God has given them a unique ministry for a specific reason. In some cases, pastors struggle to understand what the specific purpose and reason is, or should be, for them serving in their current ministry. I have spent many days as a bishop in The Lutheran Church—Missouri Synod trying to help men figure out what their purpose is in their current ministry and how to grow within that ministry.

While continuing to serve and love the people of God, effective pastoral leaders understand the purpose God has established for them in proclaiming the Gospel. Almost everyone that I have ever encountered who fulfills the Office of Public Ministry understands the critical importance of proclamation, the annunciation of the Gospel, and forgiving the sins of the penitent. Having a clear purpose in pastoral leadership helps motivate and direct the pastoral leader in his work within the office.

This reality was seen clearly when Jesus declared the purpose of Peter's leadership. Jesus declared, "And I tell you, you are Peter, and on this rock I will build My church, and the gates of hell shall not prevail against it" (Matthew 16:18). The purpose for Peter's life was for Jesus to build His Church on the witness and profession that Peter was given by the power of the Holy Spirit. The key in this passage is that the gates of hell shall not prevail against the Church. The purpose of the Gospel message is that all would hear the good news of Jesus Christ and the salvation Christ won for the world on the cross.

Satan will do everything and anything to thwart the Gospel message from going out and being fruitful. But he shall not prevail because Christ Himself established the purpose and the calling of the Office of the Holy Ministry, which is to proclaim and lead His people. As Jesus says in Matthew 9:37, "The harvest is plentiful, but the laborers are few." Christ has set apart the pastoral office to be a leadership office. The proclamation of the Gospel, the forgiveness of the penitent, and the declaration of the grace of God make up the purpose of the leadership role of the pastoral ministry. Being an effective pastoral leader means you understand the purpose that God has established for you within the Office of the Holy Ministry.

In my experience, too often men get beat up, criticized, and simply abused in their role as pastoral leaders. This causes many to forget the actual purpose for why they are a pastor in the first place. Fulfilling the role of proclaimer and providing assurance of forgiveness through the sacrifice of Christ are the central themes of the pastoral leadership office. This purpose has not changed since the time of Christ and will not until His return. As a pastoral leader, standing in the stead of Christ and by His command is a monumental responsibility.

Following Will Always Get You into Trouble

Choosing to follow as your leadership style will always get you into trouble. You must understand that those whom you follow do not have the same responsibilities that you do within the pastoral office. One clear example of this is the promise in the ordination vows to remain silent about those sins confessed to you. While God commands us not to gossip, I have never heard a layman ever commit or promise to never share those things confessed to him. Clearly, those who fulfill the pastoral office understand the critical importance of remaining silent about those things confessed. Unfortunately, the playing field is not leveled in that everyone else has not had that same commitment and promise.

Likewise, the heavy burden of carrying out the Office of the Ministry falls only on the one who is called to do so. It has become clear to me over my time as a pastor that when people want something done, they will seek to influence the pastor to accomplish their desires. Decisions often get made to satisfy the needs of individuals rather than to do what is best for the congregation and the people of God. This plays itself out in many ways within the life of the parish.

Time and again during my time as president of the English District, I have seen instances throughout the congregations in the district where lay leaders make decisions that benefit themselves. In every one of those cases, I have also witnessed a pastoral leader who followed rather than led through the Word of Christ. Because of the nature of following, in these examples every scenario ended up with a difficult, more negative outcome. Each time I have witnessed a pastoral leader simply following rather than leading, I have also seen a great deal of havoc that ensued within the life of the parish.

It can be very easy for active pastoral leaders to step aside and simply let active members accomplish things. Often in smaller congregations, the active leaders can dominate because they are the only ones willing to serve. This has caused many pastors, in my experience, to step aside and follow rather than take the reins of leadership and direct the congregation in the will of God. The temptation is always to simply let others do the job since it is less effort on the part of the pastor. This seems the route best traveled—until something goes wrong, and then the pastor is the one in the crosshairs of the rest of the congregation.

In one clear example of this, a pastor allowed a lay leader to set contracts for the congregation without any oversight. That led to the lay leader setting a contract where he got paid to do things around the church that most in the congregation thought he was volunteering for. This created great controversy within the congregation as other members started to uncover the reality that this lay leader was establishing contracts for himself and increasing the amount of money that he was paying himself. What made this situation even more dramatic was that while he was increasing his salary in his contracts to himself, he was simultaneously seeking to cut the pastor's salary because the congregation was experiencing financial difficulties.

Consistent oversight, as well as having checks and balances within the congregational setting, is a clear means to ward off problems and potential disasters. By not having a system in place that brings accountability and oversight to a congregation, pastors can find themselves in the middle of controversy. One additional issue is that people, when left unchecked, will be strongly tempted to push the boundaries within their sinful situation until they get caught or completely fail.

Take Everything into Account

If you follow a leader, you will likely, if not always, get lost in leadership. This reality must not be forgotten when you calculate the costs of leadership. Early on in my life as district president, I had a situation where a very faithful pastoral leader sought to sit back and allow his lay leaders to dictate scenarios in the congregation and with the school ministry. What he did not consider was that this was setting a tone for the remainder of his ministry within the congregation. As a passive style of leadership unfolded, a vacuum was created in the leadership position, and it became filled with the lay leader who saw the opening.

I believe that in many cases within the life of a pastoral leader, counting the full costs of every decision is overlooked for ease and expediency in any given situation. One of the hallmarks of leadership that I have been taught over my years by effective role models is to take everything into account when making decisions and acting in leadership. You cannot decide without understanding the possible ramifications in other aspects of ministry and leadership. Failing to take everything into account will cause issues at later stages in ministry.

Early in my ministry, I was very impulsive and desired to react immediately to criticisms and challenges made to me by laymen with regards to congregational leadership. But what I learned over time was that waiting and contemplating the entirety of the costs of my decision-making in the end produced better decisions. That does not always mean that every decision will take twice as long to make. In fact, in certain circumstances, decisions can be made quicker and more efficiently if you've counted all the costs and ramifications of the decision-making; you can consider and then simply make a decision and move forward.

One of the leading mentors that I have had in my life has put this reality into practice for me in many different situations. I have watched him make decisions that calculate all the costs of the specific decision at hand without losing focus on the goal and motivation for planning. I have also witnessed time and again how particularly important it is to factor in all the implications of the decisions being contemplated. That is to say, you must understand that you will always have collateral damage as you make decisions. Often, this collateral damage can be the most difficult and dramatic to deal with as you seek to lead God's people.

One technique that has had a significant impact on my leadership style is asking leaders and workers questions to set the stage for effective leadership. These might include questions about cost, time, and people involved. A good question to always ask is "Does God's Word speak to this decision? If so, what does it say?" Know as many answers as possible to these questions before you ask them. That is to say, understanding the totality and impact of the decision at hand is a crucial factor in being a successful pastoral leader. In many respects, you can build trust with those you are leading when you know the answers to the questions you ask as they pertain to the implications of the ministry and the decisions at hand.

Another aspect of this point that needs to be factored in is how to protect yourself from the influences of people who would want to lead you astray. Being aware of circumstances and issues within the ministry will prevent you from being caught off guard and flat-footed. Ultimately, this protects you from the influences of people who want you to fail. By doing the proper homework and understanding the circumstances, you can give advice and lead with integrity and honesty. These factors combine to allow you to be effective and efficient as a strong leader who has weighed all the costs and implications of each decision being made.

Don't Be Tempted to Think You Are Always Right

It is easy as a pastor to think that you are always right and always make good decisions. Because the pastoral office is highly esteemed and respected by the laity, a pastor can think that the respect is for him, rather than for the office itself. You can be lured into a false sense of admiration and reverence that is more about the office that you hold than about you. This is a false sense that some pastors simply slide into, but you must fight the urge to take compliments and instead be humble, knowing that you will make mistakes in ministry and life. Let me be clear, as I have learned repeatedly throughout my ministry: you will be wrong from time to time. Accept that reality and be ready to admit it when it occurs, without loss of confidence or integrity. It happens to all good leaders, and it will happen to you.

One important technique that effective leaders employ is to surround themselves with people who will be honest with them and not be afraid to tell them when they are wrong. Having an honest relationship with lay leaders whom you trust can be the difference between being successful or failing in ministry. I have been blessed over the years with honest congregational leaders who sought to be constructive and direct when I was not right about something in ministry. That has made my growing and learning so much easier as I recognize my mistakes and learn from my errors. Over my career, I cannot tell you the number of conversations that I have had with beloved church leaders who simply reminded me that I am human and that as hard as I try, I will always make mistakes.

Show humility when presenting your case or taking a stand within the congregation. You may very well be right about the point that you are making; however, you may be simply overconfident in your understanding, leading your members to distrust you in the process. This has been a challenge for me over the years.

I remain vigilant and watchful that I do not let my pride overtake me when I am right about a given point in leadership. Likewise, I continue to work on receiving criticism with humility and grace. This is not easy for many people to do, even though it is commanded by God as a quality of those who serve Him in the office.

I remember early on in my first congregation having to deal with a conflict situation at a sister church. The district president sent in a reconciler to listen to the members and the pastor regarding the conflict that existed within the congregation. I had the privilege of being a part of those conversations as a circuit visitor, and I marveled at how the reconciler listened to each member of the congregation talk about the past. I also remember asking the reconciler if he could teach me how to be a better listener, and his response was simply, "No." While it may seem harsh when first hearing this account, I can tell you I understood what he meant. Being an effective leader is a skill set that God gives, and it is not a skill that everyone has. While I am a firm believer that you can grow in your listening skills, I also believe that some have it as a spiritual gift and others simply do not.

Oftentimes, our zeal for service or for contributing to solving problems can cause us to not be effective listeners. I learned that early on in my ministry and have since tried to employ those techniques of being a better listener with humility whenever I am dealing with conflict or leadership situations. Being a better listener helps pastoral leaders understand how and what to answer when a question is asked. This helps the pastoral leader also understand that he will not always be right and must from time to time admit he does not have the right answer.

Conclusion

Over time, I have learned that leading, not following, is the most effective pastoral leadership technique. In fact, every week in chapel when I greet the kids as they come in, but especially when they leave, I remind them to lead not follow. By now, the young children of the church know what is meant by being a leader, not a follower. In fact, I have witnessed many situations in the school that I serve where children have been fighting to be the leader in my presence to fulfill my encouragement to not be a follower. Effective pastoral leaders will understand leading is what God calls us to do, not to follow.

Leadership, especially within a congregational setting, can be difficult at best. Leading out of fear will only cause you to make bad decisions and regret them later in your ministry. Satan would have all pastoral leaders operate out of fear rather than faith. Instead, God calls us to trust in Him and lean on His mighty power. Being an effective pastoral leader means that your decision-making will all be generated out of faith in God and love for your neighbor. Don't be fearful—be faithful.

Having a purpose and understanding the goal as a pastoral leader are crucial to success and stability within a congregation. Without a specific purpose in ministry, pastoral leaders can lose focus and be led astray, often taken completely off course. The clear purpose of Christ for His Church is to confess Him to the world, receive the forgiveness that only He can provide, and love God and neighbor without fear.

Therefore, following will always lead to being lost as you make bad decisions. One afternoon, I went into the daycare with some of the younger kids, and two of the young boys were being placed in time-out for misbehaving. When I inquired as to what was going on, the teacher informed me that one of the two young men was an absolute follower. What that meant was every time the other young man acted up inappropriately, the other young boy simply mimicked his behavior and acted in the same manner. He often got in trouble not because of what he was doing, but because he was trying to do what the other young boy was doing. Following always leads to trouble when it is not coupled with wanting to do the right thing in any given situation.

Always calculate the costs of your decisions in pastoral leadership situations. Look at the overall picture and factor in all the potential implications of your decisions. Do not make simple and easy choices without understanding how they will play out in the life of the congregation. Don't be lured into quick decisions without calculating their implications as well. Take time to think, pray, and evaluate how your decisions will impact the ministry and the congregation as a whole.

Humility is difficult for most pastoral leaders, and Satan makes that reality more difficult every day. Satan provides those in the public eye with a false sense that they are right and without mistake. This is dangerous. Do not be lured into thinking that everything you say or every position you take will be right. Be humbled to be corrected by loving faithful laymen and women when you are in the Office of the Holy Ministry. Do not be afraid to admit when you're wrong and take responsibility when needed.

REFLECTIONS

1. Do you find it easier in life to lead or follow?

   a. *Give examples of it being easier to lead.*

   b. *Give examples of it being easier to follow.*

2. While it is true that Satan will affect both the leader who likes to lead and the leader who likes to follow, each style has its benefits and its difficulties. What struggles and attacks from Satan are each style of leadership prone to have?

3. Does fear prevent you from doing the right thing as a pastoral leader?

4. What are some instances in your pastoral life where fear has overtaken you and prevented you from doing what was right?

5. What moments in your pastoral life do you look back on and regret how you handled the situation, having hindsight now of the way it turned out?

6. Give examples of times in your leadership life when you did not heed the advice of wiser people and regretted it later. Is there a way to avoid that in the future?

CHAPTER V

Acting the Part and Loving Your People

Over my years of ministry, I have been blessed to serve faithful, loving, dedicated, and educated people of God. They have been lovers of the Office of the Holy Ministry and have loved anyone occupying that office. Therefore, I have learned over the years that acting the part of a pastoral and congregational leader is essential to the success and longevity of my service in the Church. Acting the part comes in different shapes and different forms throughout the life of the pastor. Sometimes the pastoral leader needs to be the father figure, while other times he must be the listener and the therapist. Regardless of the role you are playing as a pastor, you must always remember the office in which you serve.

Being nimble on your feet as a pastoral leader will allow you to move and shift between roles and not detach yourself from the ever-present and always-constant role of a spiritual caregiver. As I said at the outset of this book, pastoral care and pastoral leadership are not in competition with each other and are never separate in the life of the pastor. Attaching everything you say and do to the proclamation of the Gospel and the forgiving of the sinner will always keep your mind and heart focused on doing God's work and not your work. Thus, you are fulfilling the call from God and the ordination vows you spoke when you declared that you would care for the young and old alike, teaching them the Word of God and forgiving those who are penitent.

Over my years as a district president, I have seen various and different ways that brothers in the ministry, men of God, were fulfilling the Office of the Holy Ministry as pastoral leaders. I have witnessed many different interpretations of acting the part and fulfilling the roles and duties of an effective pastoral leader. On some occasions, I have seen pastors who have gone overboard in emphasizing their role as the called pastor of the church. Oftentimes, this occurs in conflict situations or in authoritative wrestling matches within the congregational structure. In my experience, this never ends well for the people of God or the pastoral leader. It always leads to congregational strife and heartache.

As you carry out the functions and roles of being an effective pastoral leader within your current congregational setting, you should always keep in mind the role that God has established for you. That means you may endure periods of great difficulty and great stress. Like Joseph of the Old Testament, you may even be sold into slavery in one form or another. While inhabiting the role of the called pastor of the congregation, you still need to take the approach that Joseph himself took with his brothers when they came to Egypt needing food, all those many years after they had sold him into slavery. His reaction was nothing but love, compassion, and mercy toward the very brothers who sought to get rid of him.

What You Meant for Harm God Meant for Good

Throughout our lives, we can recall instances where great evil has been done to us. In my experience as a pastor, I have seen many times where great evil was done to the people of God, in some cases by their loved ones. I can also say that in all those situations, I saw God work some kind of good through the difficulty that was being endured. In the New Testament Book of Romans, chapter 8, we hear these words, "And we know that for those who love God all things work together for good, for those who are called according to His purpose" (Romans 8:28). This promise has been fulfilled by God time and time again in my life and the life of the Church. You are a servant of the God of our fathers, and He will always make good come from the intended evil that people seek against you in your ministry and life.

It is clear in the life of the Church that Satan would want nothing but destruction, hurt, and pain for all the children of God. This was especially true for the Old Testament figure Joseph who was sold into slavery by his brothers. There is no greater example in the Bible. It was clear that Joseph's brothers hated him because their father favored Joseph over them. In fact, the only way they felt they could deal with that reality was to kill him. But instead of killing him, they simply sold him to a caravan of traders and made it seem as if a wild animal had killed him. However, God took the tragedy that their evil intentions and selfish, hate-filled actions inflicted on their brother Joseph and turned it toward incredibly good purposes.

As if the betrayal by his brothers was not enough for Joseph, he endured several instances in his slavery that could have caused him even greater anger and hatred toward his brothers. From the beginning of his being noticed by Potiphar's wife, Joseph was constantly being bombarded and tested along his journey. Though Joseph denied the sexual advances toward Potiphar's wife, he was thrown in jail. This would cause any normal person to be overly angry at the situation. But Genesis 39:21 reminds us, "But the Lord was with Joseph and showed him steadfast love and gave him favor." God never left Joseph and was always unfolding His will in the life of Joseph.

In every instance in Joseph's life, God showed him mercy and compassion at the very deepest hour of his need. Even in the midst of the tragedies that Joseph endured, the mercy and steadfast love of God were with him always. His hand of grace and favor rested upon Joseph. Later, Joseph would have an opportunity to be compassionate toward his brothers and repay evil with love and mercy. This is a great example for any pastoral leader who endures difficulty, criticism, and malice in any other form of evil. Know that while you are in the seat of leadership, you will always be under the gun and a target for Satan—much like Joseph, whom Satan attempted to attack and destroy at every turn.

Later in Joseph's life, we have the wonderful example of his brothers during the famine needing to come to Egypt for food. It is clear in Genesis 42 that his brothers did not know him when they bowed before him requesting food. The biblical text reminds us that Joseph knew his brothers, but they did not know him. He wanted to test them and make it hard for them at the beginning of their reunion. The more interaction Joseph had with his brothers, the more his love and unity with his brothers grew.

As time moved on, Joseph's father was called to the glory of God. This caused his brothers great fear and trembling as they worried about Joseph exacting punishment upon them for their evil deeds done toward him. However, one of the greatest biblical quotes on this topic follows this interchange. In Genesis 50:20–21, we hear these words, which ring true to this very day in the lives of the people of God, "'As for you, you meant evil against me, but God meant it for good, to bring it about that many people should be kept alive, as they are today. So do not fear; I will provide for you and your little ones.' Thus he comforted them and spoke kindly to them." Joseph showed love and mercy to the very people who had hurt and betrayed him.

When evil is done to us as pastoral leaders, our first reaction ought not to be revenge and punishment. In fact, the example of Joseph should lead to both our understanding and our actions. When evil is done to us, the words of God are brought to our minds: when people seek to do evil against us, God reminds us that He will use it for His good purpose and His good pleasure for the sake of the Gospel. As an effective pastoral leader, you should always remember this Bible passage and live by it in all that you say and do, never seeking revenge or punishment but seeking the grace of God that it might be used for good.

In your life as a pastoral leader, there will be times when people will spark a visceral reaction of anger from you. Often, people will say and do things that will lead you to react in anger, and rage will be your initial response to such evil. This is a normal human reaction. However, as a pastoral leader, you must remind yourself that, like Joseph of the Old Testament, you do not need to repay evil with evil. You have the ability and the unique opportunity to share mercy, love, and grace. This is a true reflection of the ultimate sacrifice, Jesus the Savior.

Criticism Will Come, Rest Assured

If there's one thing we know about the sinful world we live in, it is that criticism will always come to those in leadership, especially those who serve in the Office of the Holy Ministry. The simple reality for any pastor is this: criticism will come, especially when you're not prepared for it. I have often been drawn into comfortable periods in my ministry and in the life of the district, and out of nowhere, difficulties and criticism come flying in. Criticism always came knocking at my door at times when I least expected it. It has always been at a moment when I was totally at peace that criticism has blindsided me and caught me off guard.

In fact, I have been in many meetings as a district president where a layperson has lashed out at the pastor and hurled some harsh and unprovoked criticisms toward him. In many of those instances, I had to call the pastor into focus prior to him trying to lay out a defense and a case to uphold his good name. Meanwhile, as the interchange between the critical layperson and the pastor carried on, most of the rest of the attendees could clearly see through what was happening and who was at fault. There was no doubt that the angry layperson was simply on the path of attack and hurt.

I remember one instance in my early ministry where a beloved member of mine was not happy with something I had said in a Bible class. He was a single man, never married, and was up in age. I'll never forget the day he continued to step into my personal space with anger and hostility, firing off insults at me because he was upset about what I had said in the Bible class. Fortunately, at the time, I had another veteran member present in the room who simply informed the person, "You'd better back off and stop moving into the pastor's space." In this case, it wasn't just the insults that he was hurling at me; it was also the invasion of my private space that caused the hair on the back of my neck to rise.

You must keep in mind that it's not always simply verbal insults that can cause you to lose your control and composure.

Criticism can come in various forms. Saying critical things is obviously the easiest form of insult that can cause you to lose your temper. But there are various other ways that laypeople can, through the temptation of Satan, cause you to lose your cool. One of the first lessons I was taught in my vicarage was this: don't allow laypeople to engage you while you are alone and may be in a vulnerable state of mind, especially when they are being critical of you. Engaging anyone, especially if they're being critical of you, almost always goes bad if you do not have complete and full control of your emotions and your actions.

Because pastoral leaders will always be targets for criticism, I would like to share with you the clear biblical passage from 1 Timothy 3:1–2, "The saying is trustworthy: If anyone aspires to the office of overseer, he desires a noble task. Therefore an overseer must be above reproach." This passage reminds us clearly that we must not allow ourselves to be dragged into battles that only glorify Satan as God's people attack one another with evil intent, malevolence, and spite. Being above reproach is the guiding principle for all pastoral leaders, especially for those who are high-quality pastoral leaders giving the correct and God-pleasing example to their laypeople.

Loving the Unlovable

It goes without saying and is in fulfillment of God's command to love your neighbor as yourself. This command of God is a simple one, and yet one that is very difficult to fulfill. In your life as a pastoral leader, it is crucial to maintain the practice of loving the people of God despite the way they act. Loving those who are critical of you or not harboring resentment against those who treat you badly can be a thorn in the flesh of God's people. When you are in the public eye, you will always and unequivocally solicit criticism and second-guessing.

When I was in high school, my pastor once told me that if I become a pastor, I must accept the fact that my people will talk about me. At the time, I wasn't sure what he meant. I didn't realize that he was talking about the fact that your laypeople will talk about you and in some cases be very critical about you as they talk to one another. I have experienced this reality over and over in my career and ministry.

I have witnessed significant violations of the Eighth Commandment when it came to my name and my service to God in the Church. It is very easy to simply let false and misleading things come to your lips as you speak about someone you have issues with. Ephesians 4:29 makes this point clear, "Let no corrupting talk come out of your mouths, but only such as is good for building up, as fits the occasion, that it may give grace to those who hear." This command is one that should be held before everyone who speaks about others in ungodly ways.

I do not believe it is an uncommon reality for pastors to be talked about by their laypeople. I do, however, believe that loving those who are unlovable is a task that all pastors must undertake. As children of the heavenly Father and inhabitants of a sinful world, we will all encounter people who are unlovable, people who simply seek to do evil, those who do not want to be reconciled or be in a harmonious relationship with God. They are simply saying, "I'm doing evil and exacting harm on people." In fact, in a recent conversation with a colleague in the ministry, I made the observation that when you're dealing with perpetually unhappy people, you must expect at all times they are scheming and plotting to do evil against you.

We can all at times be unlovable. We can all at times be so consumed with equaling the wrongs done to us that we lose sight of the exhortations of Christ. To love your neighbor as yourself must begin with loving yourself. If pastoral leaders cannot be in a harmonious and clear state of self-satisfaction and self-forgiveness, then they will never be able to love the unlovable. While I will cover this point in more depth in later chapters, I would like to simply say now that all effective pastoral leaders must have a father confessor. You must have someone to whom you can go and confess your shortcomings and failings and directly receive the absolution of Christ. This will allow you to love the unlovable. Once you receive and believe the Lord's love for you and His word of forgiveness spoken to you, you will be able to love the unlovable.

I fondly remember one of my early shut-in members reminding me that loving the unlovable is what God calls the Church to do. She reminded me that my role as a pastor was to seek those who did not want to be found. To seek after those who would not want to reconcile or be forgiven. To love those who would simply desire to harm me and anyone in the church. She went on to remind me that loving the unlovable is what Christ has done for us. This was illustrated on Good Friday when Jesus was led to the cross and the very people who just five days earlier would have heralded Jesus as the king were now calling for His crucifixion. The message that comes from the pastoral office is this: Jesus loves the unlovable.

Truly effective pastoral leaders understand the task of loving the unlovable. Effective pastoral leaders will never give up on those who refuse to love them and speak well of them. Loving pastors will always seek out the lost and the straying sheep despite the reality that the sheep will bite back. Maintaining a spirit of care, concern, and compassion for all the sheep of God, even those who are unlovable and not desirable, is the calling of the pastoral leader.

Loving in the Face of Betrayal

During my early years in the church, my family and I were members of a church that had a school. This had a profound impact on my life and service to the Church. Being able to be immersed and constantly in the Word of God was something that has been a benefit to my life and my ministry. One biblical story that stands out to me that I learned during my grade school years at a Lutheran grade school is the story of Jacob and Esau. This story is a dramatic and profound example of the betrayal of a loved one and a brother. For many, this level of betrayal is dramatic and overwhelming.

As has been said, criticism, hurt, and even betrayal will be a part of the pastoral life. What makes betrayal so much more hurtful is when it is done by somebody whom you have a deep and profound relationship with. Jacob deceived his father and then stole the blessing of his brother Esau. This is a significant biblical story, in that Jacob received the blessing from his father by stealing it and then regularly carried with him guilt until he met his brother a little over twenty years later. In fact, the biblical text tells us that Jacob feared his brother Esau's vengeance after taking the blessing. He carried with him terror and fear that his brother Esau would destroy him and his whole family because of it. And yet, later in life as Jacob drew near to Esau, he divided up his family so that in the event that Esau sought justice by attacking, half of his family would live. When Esau met up with Jacob, Genesis 33 tells us, "But Esau ran to meet him and embraced him and fell on his neck and kissed him, and they wept" (Genesis 33:4).

Esau had every right to hold and harbor anger against his brother for betraying him and stealing the blessing of the family. He had every justifiable reason to enact revenge on his brother for the evil done to him, and yet Esau's response to his brother after not seeing him for some time was joy, compassion, and tears. Even though Jacob had stolen the blessing from him, Esau maintained his love and his care for his brother, rejoicing at their reunion. This is a great symbol of forgiveness and love for a brother who had betrayed Esau. Even though his own brother betrayed him, much like in the story of Joseph, this man of God showed love to the very one who betrayed him.

In the life of every pastor, a time will come when a beloved layman or laywoman will betray him and sell him out for selfish gain. A truly beautiful and effective pastoral leader is one who can act like Esau and Joseph, who can return the evil that a family member or a loved one exacted upon him with forgiveness, mercy, and compassion. Being able to extend love to those who betrayed you in a leadership position demonstrates the calling of Christ to forgive others as you have been forgiven before God.

I can speak from experience; the greatest test of my pastoral leadership has come in dealing with people who have betrayed me and lied about me. Being able to overlook that offense as a pastor is crucial to being able to be effective in leadership. Being able to move forward and not remain captive to the hurt and pain caused by the betrayal of a loved one is a true testimony to a pastoral leader who understands forgiveness and grace from God.

Likewise, there is no greater scenario in your life as a pastor than seeing one of your laypeople repenting and being forgiven. Much like the Scriptures say, there is more joy in heaven over one sinner who repents than over one thousand who remain faithful to God. A great joy in the life of an effective pastoral leader is seeing the Holy Spirit work restoration and forgiveness when there has been a transgression and a separation between the pastor and his people. Being able to reconcile and repair a relationship that was destroyed through the trial is a great picture of the compassion and mercy that our God gave the world on Good Friday and Easter morn.

Conclusion

It is true that one of the greatest difficulties of being an effective pastoral leader and carrying out the functions of the office is being able to love your people in the face of their betrayal and hurt. Being caring to those who hate you is a problem for pastors, as it is for the world. Seeking to be in a right relationship with God's people even when they hurt you is what being a servant leader is all about. Much like Jesus during Palm Sunday's ride toward Jerusalem, pastors must look in the face of people who cheer them on, knowing that they will be the very people who speak evil against them later.

As a pastoral leader, I would continue to highlight the importance of anyone within the office having a Joseph-like approach to ministry. Remember the words of Joseph to his brothers: "What you meant for evil, God turned to good." It is very difficult for humans to understand that God's exacting judgment might not be something we are able to see with our own eyes. Sometimes it's important for us to simply understand that God will work good from any and all evil that is done to us as effective pastoral leaders. Not seeking to enact our own justice, especially when we are in a position of authority, is a key hallmark of being a high-quality pastoral leader.

Unfortunately, the old saying is true: criticism will come when we least expect it. That should not deter you from doing your job or from leading from the pastoral office. It is important to remember, however, that when you are at your most comfortable point, likely that is when Satan will strike, using laypeople to be critical and hurtful. But remember that exacting justice against those who are critical only plays into Satan's temptations. Simply understanding and realizing that criticism will come (and when it does, not letting it destroy you) is a key factor to being successful as a pastoral leader.

One important task for the pastoral leader is to love the unlovable. Just because there will be many within your own ministry who will be difficult to love because of their behavior and actions does not give you the excuse to not love them. Simply using the excuse that people themselves are unlovable does not free you from carrying out your vocation as a pastoral leader. Turning away from extending compassion, forgiveness, and love to unlovable people is unacceptable through the Office of the Holy Ministry. One of the great abilities that God gives to us in the Church is to love the unlovable as He does for you and for me daily.

There is no doubt about it—being betrayed by someone you care about or one of your loved ones is the ultimate pain in the life of any person. Like Joseph and Esau in the Old Testament stories, being betrayed by brothers and sisters and loved ones can leave a long-lasting effect and deep scars in the lives of people. However, using the same examples of Joseph and Esau, we understand that forgiving our loved ones and moving forward in grace and love is what God calls us to do. The stories of Joseph and Esau, being betrayed by their brothers remind us as pastoral leaders that anyone can sin against us and hurt us, even those who are our brothers and sisters. Remain vigilant and understand this is Satan at work in the life of the Church. Forgive and restore as Joseph and Esau did in their biblical stories in the Old Testament.

REFLECTIONS

1. List times in your life when you felt that you were doing what God was asking of you and you still were not making progress in your work.

   a. *In how many of those instances did you receive criticism for what you were doing?*

   b. *Did you feel like it was hopeless to carry on with the tasks you were doing for the Lord and the Church?*

2. Read Genesis 50:19–21, "But Joseph said to them, 'Do not fear, for am I in the place of God? As for you, you meant evil against me, but God meant it for good, to bring it about that many people should be kept alive, as they are today. So do not fear; I will provide for you and your little ones.' Thus he comforted them and spoke kindly to them."

   a. *Have you had moments in your life when people meant their actions for your harm and God used them for His good?*

   b. *Discuss how you can help others with their struggles when people intentionally harm them.*

   c. *How can you support them in their struggle?*

   d. *Criticism will always come; how can you deal with criticism in a God-pleasing manner and without allowing anger to overcome you?*

3. Matthew 5:44–48 states, "But I say to you, Love your enemies and pray for those who persecute you, so that you may be sons of your Father who is in heaven.

For He makes His sun rise on the evil and on the good, and sends rain on the just and on the unjust. For if you love those who love you, what reward do you have? Do not even the tax collectors do the same? And if you greet only your brothers, what more are you doing than others? Do not even the Gentiles do the same? You therefore must be perfect, as your heavenly Father is perfect."

a. *Do you pray for your enemies and ask God to bless them?*

b. *What is the motivation for doing this when someone has hurt you?*

c. *As a pastoral leader, what are some ways you can show kindness to those who persecute you?*

4. How can you deal with those who betray you in the Office of the Pastoral Ministry?

5. Do you have people in your life who are hard to love?

6. What do you do to deal with those types of people?

CHAPTER VI

Responsibilities in the Office of Pastoral Leader

High-quality pastoral leaders understand clearly that taking responsibility for every aspect of ministry is important because the pastor will be held accountable for all successes and failures within the ministry. Therefore, effective pastoral leaders know they should always pay attention to all aspects of congregation life and ministry. Whether they delegate responsibilities to those within the congregation or assign them to other church workers, pastoral leaders are ultimately responsible and must remain engaged in all aspects of pastoral leadership.

Even though it is impossible for one person to do everything within the life of a ministry, it is important that all pastoral leaders understand that they must take responsibility for all things within the ministry. It is easy to blame someone else when something within the life of the ministry does not work out—after all, remember the Genesis account with Adam when he blamed Eve for the sin of eating from the tree of the knowledge of good and evil. The natural reaction is to point the finger at someone else. But high-quality pastoral leaders will never point the finger at someone else; they will always take responsibility for things that go on.

Unfortunately, other leaders within the congregation will tend to blame different members when things go awry or when problems occur. One example of this that I have encountered often as a pastor and a district president is in the area of trusteeship within a congregation. Some of the greatest congregational leaders that I have worked with have been the heads of trustees at the congregations I have served. Likewise, some of the most difficult people I have dealt with are heads of trustees at congregations in the district that I've served.

People love to take credit when things are going great and smooth; however, they love to blame other people when there are difficulties and problems. There are also two different schools of thought when it comes to leading and having responsibilities. You can desire the title and all that goes along with it, or you can ensure that the job gets done effectively and efficiently no matter who takes credit for it being completed. Being an effective leader requires the ability to ensure that other people will complete the tasks they were entrusted with, and that they do the tasks at a high level.

Good leaders understand clearly that they are responsible even when someone else is doing the work. Therefore, having people who are trustworthy and able to complete the tasks that they say they will do is crucial for any effective leader. Placing trustworthy and competent people around you can be the difference between being successful as a pastoral leader or not.

There Is More to Leadership Than the Title

Being in charge is appealing to many people. Unfortunately, many people who want to be in charge do not fully understand the burdens that go along with being responsible. Unequivocally, there is more to being a leader and in charge than just being able to say you're the boss. A title brings with it a certain level of authority and responsibility. The person behind the title understands that leading has nothing to do with having a title. Too often in my career, I have come across those who have a title but are simply not leaders. Conversely, one can be a leader without a title and serve faithfully and effectively throughout his or her life in ministry.

One of the greatest lessons I have learned from some of those who have held the highest of titles in their organization is simply this: helping others be successful and not being afraid of them getting the credit is the sign of a great leader. Too often in our selfish and sinful lives, we seek the credit for every good thing that occurs in the life of a congregation or ministry. We likewise do not want to bear responsibility when things do not go well. There is no doubt in my mind that helping others become successful within your organization is one of the greatest tasks that an effective leader can perform. Simply put, don't be afraid to let others get credit for their successes in ministry. Encourage and uplift others as they serve in order for your ministry to enjoy success and sustainability.

As a leader, I know it can become very easy to look at the little circumstances and the daily problems that occur rather than the big picture. I have always looked at the big picture of any given situation rather than the small circumstances of today. While the circumstances of today matter and should be dealt with faithfully and pointedly, I do believe that more leaders must look at the bigger picture and the implications on the overall ministry when it comes to leading others.

It is very important to see every decision that you make as a piece of the overall puzzle. Managing people and circumstances is difficult on a good day, so I would strongly recommend that every decision that is made should fit into an overall theme, mission, and goal. Nothing should be done independent of supporting the ministry and the mission of your organization without considering its connectivity to the overall puzzle. Too often, pastors get caught up in the nuances of the specific small situation and forget about the connective tissues that those small situations have to the overall picture and ministry of the congregation.

One of the key elements of being a leader is to help others understand why you are doing what you're doing and its importance in fitting into the overall mission of the ministry. Every activity that is done, from worship to social ministries outside the congregation, centers around the life of the faithful in service and love to Christ. Each individual situation plays a part in connecting the congregation and individuals to the overall ministry and mission of the congregation. The little things do absolutely matter, and they should always be seen in the context of the overall big picture. Effective leaders will always make the connection between the two without making them be in competition with each other.

Participation Is an Essential Element of Leadership

One element of successful pastoral leadership must always be participation as the pastoral leader. One of the natural instincts that I had going into the ministry was a desire to be physically involved with the work of the church, especially the physical work of the church. That is to say, I love doing maintenance-type work around the church with members of the congregation. This was both from a team-building perspective and also from a leadership perspective. A pastor who does not participate in the physical work of the church stands out in a negative way to his members as the leader who tells others what to do but does not do it himself. This type of pastoral leader will rarely—if ever—garner the respect or trust of his people. Rolling up your sleeves to paint the walls and jumping on the tractor to cut the grass are great ways to demonstrate your love and commitment to the people of God where you serve.

It has been evident to me over my time as bishop and president that the pastor who does not help or participate in the physical life of the church outside of worship and Bible study sends an unspoken message to his people that he is either better than them or much different than them. That is simply not the message that a pastor should send to his people. In fact, on vicarage I was exposed to rural America in South Dakota and joyfully had the pleasure of spending many days helping members of the congregation do work around their farms and homes. It was not only a time to show love, care, and compassion to the people of God who I served, it was also a bonding experience with the members of the church. I can say joyfully that to this day I still go back to South Dakota and spend time with the members I helped while on vicarage.

Of the most pointed leadership lessons that I learned from a pastor was a negative lesson that has stuck with me since that time. I watched a parish pastor whom I looked up to say in a public meeting, "My job is to preach, teach, and visit occasionally. My job is not to sweep the floors and do the dishes." This had such a profound impact on me as I watched the faces of the people of God in this congregation and felt the absolute frustration and anger that they had toward their pastor. Without a doubt, the message he sent that day was that he was better than them and that what they were doing was beneath him. I do not take any joy in saying that the congregation imploded shortly after that interchange between the pastor and his congregation.

Another negative pastoral example came in my second year as bishop when visiting a congregation. I witnessed the pastor show up one hour after the event started and leave one hour before it ended, never assisting with setup or cleanup. In fact, I had members come up to me and ask if it was normal for a pastor to come to an event late, leave early, and not help clean up. Of course, I had to answer with no, in large part because I was there forty minutes before the event occurred and I helped set up, as well as stay and clean up. Keep in mind that I was a guest and a visitor of this event. And just like the first example, this congregation also had great difficulty and great consternation shortly after my visit because many members saw a man who was not even their pastor doing the work of the pastor.

Leading Means Taking a Stand That Others May Not Like

In the life of an effective pastoral leader, there will inevitably come times when making a decision or taking a stand will be offensive to others within the congregation. I have witnessed time and time again in my ministry and in the life of the parishes I've served in the English District where good pastors have taken a stand on a given issue within the congregation, and it causes conflict. While this fact might not be new to you, I believe that it needs to be clearly articulated. Most often in the life of a pastor, he will take a stand against something that for the world is not an issue; however, it is a biblical point, and his stance will be offensive to the world around him.

Throughout my career, I have run into one specific topic that has caused great conflict in my own congregations where I have served and in the life of the church under my supervision. From my vicarage to the present day, I have had to deal with the topic of cohabitation and its effect on the life of Christian people. This is one example where the pastoral office takes a strong biblical stand defending the Word of God as clear and concise regarding the topic of marriage and living together before marriage. Problematic in the life of Christian people is that the world does not see cohabitation as an issue or wrong in any way.

This issue has affected me both personally and professionally as I have had to deal with many people whom I love dearly and care about deeply, and yet, I have had to stand firm on my position that living together before marriage is not acceptable in the eyes of God. Thankfully, in most of the cases in my pastoral life and personal life, I have been able to navigate those waters in a loving way that did not ultimately cause separation in the relationship between the people of God and myself. But there have been those cases both personally and professionally where I have had negative interactions with people regarding the topic of cohabitation.

I understand for many veteran pastors this reality is clear and understandable as men reflect on their ministry and life of service. Unfortunately, serving as pastoral leaders requires us to take a stand on biblical principles. The world has defied God's commands and sees nothing wrong with blatant and egregious sinful behavior. This is where effective pastoral leadership collides with popular culture. Taking a stand on all biblical issues that are relative to the life of the Christian is critical for effective pastoral leaders. Difficulty must not hinder them from carrying out their service and work to God in the church. "Stand firm!" must be the call for all pastoral leaders, even in the face of great stress and difficulty.

The Word of God Is Foundational

One of the great Reformation principles of Martin Luther is *sola scriptura* (Scripture alone). This foundational principle for the Church is an important key element for effective pastoral leadership. It is the centerpiece of responsibility for all those who serve in the Office of the Holy Ministry and lead God's people. Likewise, it ought to be the foundational principle in every decision-making and behavioral activity that you would do as an effective leader. In the twenty-first century, several key biblical issues have collided with societal norms that have caused difficulty in congregations and families throughout the church.

One of the most pertinent public issues that faces the church today is abortion. The clear biblical stand on abortion is pointed: abortion is unacceptable and is the killing of unborn children. For fifty years, abortion has been considered acceptable and legal in the United States, and this has caused a great collision between scriptural fidelity and societal practice. Thankfully, this has recently been overturned by the United States Supreme Court. But in these last years, any pastor faithful to the biblical position against abortion has taken social hits and criticisms because of society's acceptance of this unbiblical practice. Every pastor I have known in my life who stands for the biblical position of life as it begins with the conception of an unborn infant has been criticized and ostracized for their position.

Nonetheless, faithful pastors have stood in defense of the unborn and against the barbaric practice of abortion in the face of criticism and mockery. Being a responsible pastoral leader means clinging to the biblical foundation of Scripture and letting those foundational principles dictate our teaching and our action, regardless of the criticism that may come. The Bible is foundational to both our beliefs and our practice, regardless of what the societal norms may be. This is the centerpiece of pastoral care as pastoral leadership in our church today.

Other more recent events have occurred in the life of the church that have demonstrated the same collision point that abortion has had since 1973. One such example of cultural collisions in church ministry is the governmental overreach during the COVID-19 pandemic that required churches to shut down and not worship. This is a perfect example of what happens when God's Word collides and impacts with popular opinion and cultural norms. Those pastors who insisted on remaining open were criticized both by members of their own congregation and by local officials for not obeying the governmental commands. These pastors believed in adherence to the Third Commandment over and above what the local government decreed and commanded.

Remaining faithful to teaching the foundational principles of the Bible has remained at the highest level of importance in the life of many of the effective pastoral leaders in my life and in the life of the church.

Another issue that has caused many pastors to be criticized and ostracized is how they have dealt with the LGBTQ issues of society today. Sexuality in the Bible is a gift from God; male and female distinctions are intended by God for the blessing of one another and the procreation of children. This is an issue that the church stands strongly on. Pastors who stand firmly in the foundational principles of sexuality and the distinctiveness of gender identity as male and female are called bigots and detached from society. Faithfulness and adherence to the Word of God require all pastors to stand firm on the biblical foundational principle of God creating man and woman distinctively to come together in one flesh within marriage for the procreation of children. This biblical principle, while simple and precise, has caused great separation and difficulty for many effective pastoral leaders.

One key point that needs to be spoken at this time is how pastors go about dealing with these societal issues in the life of leadership in the congregation. I have always said and will continue to say, stand firm under the biblical principles and foundational guidance of the Holy Scriptures. It is equally important to also be compassionate and caring with those you serve without waffling on the content of your biblical understanding. Some of the most effective pastoral leaders understand this and are masters at loving the people they serve while standing firm on the biblical principles of life, human sexuality, and our physical lives in this world.

Being an effective pastoral leader requires us to be decisive and strong without being arrogant and cocky as we serve the people of God with love and compassion. The calling of the effective pastoral leader is to remain firmly set in the foundational principles of the Bible and lovingly articulate those to the people of God. At this point, I would also like to say that pastoral leaders should not seek or pick fights on any of these controversial social issues. Likewise, they should not wither away from the conversation or discussion of these issues out of fear of criticism or attack. Maintaining a Christlike attitude and compassionate heart for those who are struggling with positions that are not congruent with the Word of God is the task of the faithful pastoral leader. Being long-suffering and loving toward those whom you serve will help to focus on the mercy, care, and compassion of Christ in the life of these people.

Criticism Is Not Always about You as a Leader

While serving as a pastor, I have come across instances in my life where I have been criticized for the position that I've taken or the responsibility to the office that I have adhered to. In many of my early years, I would react very negatively toward criticism out of feelings of inadequacy and defensiveness. It is very hard to hear criticism about yourself, especially when it is unjust and not true. Throughout my career as a district president, I have talked to pastors who have wanted to simply fight back against criticism because what was being said was untrue. This is a normal and natural reaction to criticism. It is important that all who seek to be effective pastoral leaders must understand that criticism is not always about you or your leadership style. Sometimes people will simply complain, regardless of what you say or what you do. This is a reality that every pastoral leader will face throughout his career and life in ministry.

In most of the conflict situations that I have dealt with as a district president, I have encountered church workers who immediately become angry and react with a visceral response to lies and criticism, rather than react with a patient and measured response. While this is an understandable reaction, it is simply a continuation of Satan dividing God's people and causing separation among brothers and sisters. True reconciliation can never happen unless both parties are willing to forgive and move forward in the grace of God and in His mercy. Getting angry prevents that from happening on every front and by everyone involved.

It is clear to me that Satan will always use your personal inadequacies and your failures from a human perspective to allow others to attack. This seems especially true when other bad things are occurring in the life of the parish and in your personal life. In some respects, this is also a natural reaction within the world: people tend to pile on when things are going bad in their lives. On one of my trips to Africa, I witnessed a wildebeest being attacked and eaten by a pride of lions. The clear principle that I came away with from that trip was that the strong and agile wildebeest was not the one that the lions attacked or ate. In fact, in every case while I was in Kenya, I witnessed the lame or sick, the inferior or meek being the target of the predators. This principle is one that plays out in the lives of people as well. The strong and confident leaders have fewer situations where they are attacked by the lions and the wolves. Be confident in who you are and in the place where God has called you. Keep your head held high and know that since Christ is with you, who can be against you?

I believe wholeheartedly that criticism of those who serve in leadership, especially those in the Office of the Public Ministry, occurs more often when weakness or difficulty is occurring in the life of a leader. Satan understands that when you are struggling, attacks are more effective and can do more damage, much like the scene I saw on the plains of Kenya. The effective leader needs to remember that when difficulty is occurring, any form of criticism is much more likely to cause you to react in anger. Therefore, be diligent to always respond to criticism with love and kindness.

I learned a great lesson from a seasoned pastor early on in my ministry. When laymen and women came into his office to complain, often the things that they were complaining about were not their real issue at all. In fact, oftentimes there was a hidden and more difficult issue that loomed below the surface. At the heart and root of any criticism can be anger and frustration at other issues, allowing for the current situation to merely be a springboard rather than a centerpiece. This lesson has been a valuable tool in my pastoral toolbox throughout my career. Understanding that people likely have other issues going on when they're criticizing you helps me to deal with the people of God with love and compassion.

Another aspect of this reality comes in the clear understanding that when people of God are angry at God, their closest representative of God is their pastor. This allows the laity within the congregation to take out frustrations and anger on their pastor that likely are directed toward God Himself. Throughout my career as a parish pastor and my work as a district president, I have seen this time and time again, and I understand where a person may subconsciously be sucked into criticizing the pastor when his or her frustration and anger are directed at God Himself.

Conclusion

There are clearly many responsibilities that lie with those who serve in the Office of Public Ministry. Taking responsibility for everything within the ministry is a significant cross that pastoral leaders bear as they serve God in the Church. Not being afraid of those responsibilities and dealing with them without fear are two important tasks of the effective pastor. Being invested in ministry and congregational life is one key element of being responsible as the pastoral leader and chief shepherd of the flock of Christ in that place.

Having the title of pastor is an honor and a privilege, not a right. Understanding that there is more to leading God's people than having the title is a key component to success in the Office of the Ministry. Having a title and carrying out the responsibilities of the office are two separate things. Remember not to allow the title to cause you to be puffed up; rather, it ought to remind you of the significant burden that you bear in leadership when someone calls you their pastor. There is no higher calling in the world than serving God and the Church as a pastor.

Being an effective leader means at times you will have to take a stand that is unpopular with people. Do not be afraid to take a stand for the sake of the Gospel. Understand that societal norms will collide with biblical precedent and biblical principles. Remaining faithful to the Word of God and the Church's confessions is the calling of the effective pastoral leader. Do not be afraid or wither under the pressure of societal criticism when it comes to the positions you take for the sake of the Gospel and the Church.

Every aspect of life and ministry for the pastoral leader is centered on and grounded in the Word of God. There is never a situation where the fundamental principle of biblical understanding is superseded by societal norms. Every decision that you make and every action that you take should be rooted in the Scriptures and the commands of Christ. The forgiveness of sins and salvation in Jesus Christ form the centerpiece of all public proclamations of the Church and of the pastoral leader.

It is critically important to remember that criticism you receive in the Office of the Ministry is not always about you. Oftentimes, people have frustration and anger with God and have no other place to communicate that frustration than to the pastor. Work diligently to not allow criticism to overcome you and cause you to react in anger and defensiveness. The task of an effective pastoral leader is to read his people and understand that their frustration and anger are not always necessarily directed at him or about him.

REFLECTIONS

1. Have you had moments where you felt that you were being accused by members or people for no reason and wanted to just walk away? Discuss what the Bible says about those moments and how Christ provides for you in the hour of your greatest need.

2. List points in your life and ministry when you have found yourself struggling under the burden of defending the Word of God.

   a. *What was the outcome?*

   b. *How did the situation get resolved?*

3. Discuss these Bible passages and how they apply to the situations we have discussed in this chapter.

   a. James 1:2–4, "Count it all joy, my brothers, when you meet trials of various kinds, for you know that the testing of your faith produces steadfastness. And let steadfastness have its full effect, that you may be perfect and complete, lacking in nothing."

   b. 1 Peter 5:10, "And after you have suffered a little while, the God of all grace, who has called you to His eternal glory in Christ, will Himself restore, confirm, strengthen, and establish you."

   c. Romans 12:12, "Rejoice in hope, be patient in tribulation, be constant in prayer."

   d. 1 Corinthians 10:13, "No temptation has overtaken you that is not common to man. God is faithful, and He will not let you be tempted beyond your ability, but with the temptation He will also provide the way of escape, that you may be able to endure it."

e. Romans 5:3–5, "Not only that, but we rejoice in our sufferings, knowing that suffering produces endurance, and endurance produces character, and character produces hope, and hope does not put us to shame, because God's love has been poured into our hearts through the Holy Spirit who has been given to us."

f. Exodus 14:14, "The Lord will fight for you, and you have only to be silent."

g. Philippians 4:6–7, "Do not be anxious about anything, but in everything by prayer and supplication with thanksgiving let your requests be made known to God. And the peace of God, which surpasses all understanding, will guard your hearts and your minds in Christ Jesus."

h. 1 Peter 4:12, "Beloved, do not be surprised at the fiery trial when it comes upon you to test you, as though something strange were happening to you."

4. Take time to reflect on these passages so they become a part of all your thinking and processing when you are having difficulties and trials in your life and ministry.

CHAPTER VII

Communication as a Pastoral Leader

The speed and frequency of communication today in the modern electronic age is fast-paced and direct. Mere seconds can elapse between events and their reporting on various platforms throughout the electronic sphere. Communication and clarity within communication have become a hallmark of successful organizations and individuals. By tapping into this reality that all members and potential members of congregations are living with, pastoral leaders can take advantage of the fast-paced and frequent communication streams that are existing in our society today.

Communication from the position of leadership is critical for success and for accomplishing the mission of the ministry you serve. While that statement might seem like it's purely common sense, it is much more difficult than you would expect when it comes to being in the seat of leadership. Clear and concise communication is not always the easiest when dealing with a myriad of situations within congregational ministry. Oftentimes, dealing with difficult situations makes communicating even more difficult and stressful. Nonetheless, being clear and concise with the information needed by those in the ministry or the congregation can be the difference between success and failure as a pastoral leader.

Historically, within the church, a monthly newsletter has been the traditional pattern of communicating with the people of God within a given congregation. This was and in some cases still is the preferred method of communication from the pastoral office to the congregation and membership of a church. While I do not believe that there is anything wrong with a monthly newsletter in its standard format, I do believe that simply communicating on a monthly basis can leave members with concern, wondering what is happening within the ministry on a day-to-day basis.

Upon being elected bishop and president of the English District, I made a strategic change in communication with the district pastors and congregations that proved to be a very wise one. By eliminating the monthly newsletter titled *The English Channels* and moving to a weekly communication called *Servant-2-Servant*, I was able to keep people tightly connected to the happenings of the district and congregations within the fellowship throughout the United States. This subtle change from monthly to weekly communication has created a culture of more up-to-date laity and clergy. It has also created anticipation on the part of the readers for the Friday noon communication that comes out from the district office weekly.

Besides the weekly communication that is sent out every Friday, we daily send out prayer requests for individual congregations and church workers. By utilizing Facebook, Twitter, and Instagram, we are able to connect people quickly and directly to a prayer ministry for the churches and servants throughout our district and synod in a timely fashion. This, too, has been a tremendous blessing for those who follow the district and our congregations within the LCMS.

Clarity in Communication

What is worthy of communicating to those you serve within the congregation and ministry? This can be the most important point when dealing with being a communicator as a pastoral leader. A delicate balance exists between the need to send out communication and the desire to simply communicate. There are those specific information pieces that must be articulated in a timely fashion and without delay. For example, when the church or a function at church is canceled because of weather or loss of power at the facility, an immediate clear announcement ought to be sent to those within the congregation and those attending the event.

It is also very important within your communication to help people understand what you are trying to communicate and why. Being direct and pointed helps people understand the reason for the communication and the content that is being communicated. Frequent and clear communication will always build trust and allow the pastoral leader to demonstrate his care for those he is serving within the ministry.

Clear communication allows the reader to finish the entirety of the communication, whereas unclear communication encourages the reader to simply disregard what is being said, especially if it doesn't pertain to him or her. Too often, I receive communications from people seeking to sell me their business or service, and they spend way too much time on elongated explanations of who they are and why they are sending their email or making their phone call. I get the sense they are diverting the communication in an attempt to get my mind off the sales pitch or request. This leads me to frustration and, in some cases, anger. The same thought should be applied to church communications. Get to the point and make it clear and relatable to the reader. Do not waste people's time with elongated and nonsensical lead-in paragraphs that only help your ego and do nothing for the reader receiving the information.

By remaining focused and making the communication understandable and direct, you allow the reader and the listener to engage in what is being communicated. This will allow for effective and efficient communication without distracting and frustrating your people.

Another reason for clarity in communication is the amount of time that is saved by your readers and listeners. Time is valuable to everyone, and as responsibility grows and tasks increase, the effective leader and his people will need clarity and timeliness to work together. If you are clear in your communication, you can avoid spending additional time later trying to explain what you were trying to say previously. Too often in my ministry life, I have seen people waste inordinate amounts of time trying to explain some misunderstanding. This has caused anger and frustration in almost every situation, which has often led to conflict throughout the membership of the congregation. If you use your precious time effectively up front and clarify your communication, you will always save that time in the end by avoiding confusion and frustration.

Understanding within Communication

One of the greatest issues that I have when receiving communications is not fully understanding what the writer is trying to communicate. Oftentimes, I am frustrated reading extended communications that are filled with information not related to that which the writers are trying to communicate. One of my professors in seminary used to tell us repeatedly during class, "Get to the point." It was somewhat comical during my seminary education to watch him do that to classmates who would drone on and talk without a point. I quickly understood his frustration after taking leadership in the role of bishop and president. People tend not to get to the point and are afraid of what they are trying to communicate.

It is important to make sure that the reader can easily understand what you are trying to communicate in any given communication. In order to create an environment of transparency, being clear and making the communication understandable will be the difference between the reader completing the communication or disregarding it. Help the reader or hearer feel comfortable with what he or she is receiving in any given communication. Whether you are writing an email, letter, or public statement, you must always be clear and give as much information as possible regarding the situation you are attempting to communicate to the hearer.

It can become too easy to simply make a direct statement without context or understanding. The old adage still holds weight today: honesty is the best policy, especially when dealing with communication. This truth will pay dividends when trying to communicate any number of things to the hearer or listener.

It can become difficult to communicate information that people need in order to deal with life situations when you know that some information can be offensive to them. Whether sending an email, writing a letter, or preaching a sermon, the pastoral leader must always keep in mind the information he is communicating and how those who hear it or read it are likely to receive that information. Regarding the medium of preaching as a means of communication, the preacher can be straightforward and still engaging to the listener while getting the direct and sometimes offensive legalistic point across from the Scriptures. While effective and successful preachers make this look easy, this style of communication is not always easy to pull off and, in some cases, can backfire even with the most skilled preachers. Likewise, with written communication, you must spend time crafting what you say so that understanding is had by the listener or the reader at the end of your communication.

By having an understanding of the communication style you use and the frequency with which you communicate, you are able to demonstrate empathy and compassion to those with whom you are trying to communicate. I have seen this throughout my ministry—people can be motivated in a very positive way through your understanding of communication, or they can be completely turned off and frustrated by what you have said. Even if you had no intention to frustrate people, you can quickly find yourself in a place where people are unmotivated and uninspired to participate in that which you are trying to communicate.

Always present a clear and compassionate form of communication regardless of the content you are trying to share. Compassion and understanding within communication oftentimes will generate positive feelings and connectivity to the initiative or situation you are dealing with. Congregation members want to have connectivity to what is going on and knowledge of what is occurring. Take, for example, a prayer chain. You can effectively and quickly connect a number of members to care for their brother or sister in Christ by engaging them in a prayer request for people who are going through difficult times, health crises, grief, or thanksgiving for what God has done in their lives and through them.

Using Repetition

Using repetition as a means of communicating has historically been very effective and successful. When I was contemplating going to seminary, my pastor instructed me on the preaching style that he was taught in the early 1970s. He simply said, "Tell them what you have to say, tell them what you said, and remind them of the points you were making." This style of repetition in a sermon has been a classic form used for retention and clarity within the historic office of preaching. The way we use repetition in the homiletical realm should not be ignored in all our general communications either.

The dictionary defines *repetition* as "a motion or exercise that is repeated." This repeating of the information that you desire to communicate will become solidified in the hearer or listener over time. One significant issue with using repetition in your regular communication to your congregants or your ministry partners is attempting to communicate the same information in a slightly different way to allow for engagement by the hearer or listener. The regular rhythm of communicating with your people, whether on a daily, weekly, or monthly basis, will help to create trust and connectivity with those you serve.

Being regular in your repetition and pattern of communication helps people to prepare for and anticipate what is coming. I have had many people within my own congregation and throughout the district make positive comments about the regularity and repetition of the communication that I have with those I serve. People know that the information they are seeking will be given at the appropriate time. There aren't large gaps between the communication periods of when information needs to be given and when it is received by the members of the district.

Using repetition to communicate a difficult topic can also be a means of effective leadership. What I mean by this is that when I deal with a difficult topic or circumstance, I often use a push-pull method of repetition in communication. That is to say, I introduce the topic and then leave it alone. I then return to the topic a short time later to discuss it further. I finally bring it back up after another short interval of time, in order for people not to be shocked or taken off guard by hearing it for the first time.

By introducing a difficult topic several times before acting on it, people can get used to the gravity or difficulty being discussed without becoming overly emotional. Oftentimes, this is done with the visioning process and the planning process within a congregation. When laying out grandiose ideas that can be somewhat controversial, the effective leader can communicate using repetition on the topic as a means of getting those he serves used to the topic at hand. This is where repetition can become your friend in leadership rather than a hindrance or an irritation. Allowing for feedback, questions, and discussions without action will likely lead to a more successful transition when dealing with any situation with gravity or difficulty.

Regarding repetition, one area to keep in mind is the frequency with which you repeat something. Too much repetition can be difficult for people to deal with and can cause irritation, frustration, and anger. Being strategic about when and where you place the repetition of the information you are trying to communicate can be the difference between hearers or listeners becoming upset and frustrated or them listening and being more understanding on the topic. Over time, effective leaders can read the people they serve and know how far to take the push-pull method of communicating difficult topics. People tend to be more receptive when dealing with difficult topics if they have time to process and think about things.

Helping Others Become Effective in Communication

Effective communication does not solely belong to the pastoral office as a form of leadership. The effective pastoral leader should spend time helping those he serves to improve their leadership style as well. This includes empowering other leaders within the congregation or ministry to be clear and concise in their communication style and efforts. The pastoral leader will inevitably be tied into and have responsibility for others within the congregation and how they communicate. This is one reason an effective pastoral leader needs to help empower other leaders to be successful in their communication style and effort as well.

By helping others be clear and transparent in their communication to the congregation and ministry, the effective pastoral leader creates an environment and a culture within the ministry that breeds success and trust. Simply put, ineffective or bad communication within a ministry setting can cause unnecessary and dramatic difficulties that could simply be avoided with regular, clear, and effective communication with the congregation. I have witnessed too often within my own congregation and within those I've served as bishop and president of the English District incidences where poor communication unintentionally caused dramatic and significant conflict.

On the other hand, I have witnessed several instances where intended inflammatory and offensive communication was used to generate conflict and frustration. This is never productive in any setting, let alone within the congregational setting of the church. Intentionally using communication as a means to be mean or rude is simply unacceptable. I often encounter this when dealing with frustrated laymen or women who find themselves in a difficult situation within the parish. I find myself having to be a teacher and a soundboard for those who simply want to say the most expeditious and inflammatory comment to get the point across, regardless of the damage or the wake that they leave behind.

Empowering others within the congregation to be effective in their communication will only help the ministry move forward in joy and thanksgiving. Taking seriously the role of empowering others to be effective communicators is also a significant portion of the responsibility that any effective pastoral leader has in his role. Combining his own clarity and pointedness in communication with helping others to be clear in their communication, the pastoral leader can help a congregation in ministry move forward harmoniously, serving and loving his neighbor.

Overcommunicate as a Means of Transparency

In my experience, overcommunicating information is far better than under-communicating it. People can get tired of hearing the same thing again; however, people become infuriated by not hearing the information the first time or not hearing it enough. One technique that has been taught to me over time by effective leaders is to overcommunicate with clarity rather than under-communicate with distrust. One of the specific goals of clear and concise communication is to keep people informed and updated. In my pastoral life, I have felt no greater frustration than finding out that one of my members has been in the hospital and has not told me about it. This has caused me great feelings of guilt and frustration, because had I known the member was in the hospital I would have gone and visited. I am sure anyone who has served in the Office of the Holy Ministry can empathize with this example and understand clearly why communication, especially about being in the hospital, is so critically important from a leadership perspective.

Anger, hurt, and frustration well up when a person is ill-informed, misinformed, or simply uninformed. The classic phrase spoken by many people, "If I had only known," is a statement that we all can relate to and understand. Possessing knowledge and understanding about any given situation is so important to be able to react in response to what is going on. In my experience, people feel more comfortable when they know what is happening rather than having to guess what is going on. Simply being informed and updated regarding a situation or a circumstance that affects you is a crucial element to having contentment and refraining from frustration and anger.

Going back to an earlier section in this chapter, weekly communication with similar information works best when it runs between five and seven weeks consecutively. The reason for this is very clear: people tend not to commit to memory those things that are not repeated and oftentimes disregard what they hear unless it's heard many times. I have often heard marketers talk about the magic number of seven as a marker for how many times people need to hear the same thing before they desire to investigate it themselves. This is one of the clear reasons why overcommunicating information from the leadership position is critically important for the effective pastoral leader. People tend to connect to an event or a need after repeated communications on the topic.

It should also be noted here that people can receive over-communication regarding any specific situation or event within the life of the church and still find a way to complain about not knowing what was going on. This happened to me early on in my ministry. We advertised an event that was coming up in the life of the church for approximately eight weeks, and I still had a member call me the day before, furious that he did not know this was occurring and had a scheduling conflict in his life that was going to prevent him from attending. After all, it is always the fault of the communicator if people don't get the information that they need or want.

Technology has assisted in this repetition and communication endeavor for congregations and leaders throughout the country. By having calendar reminders and repeat announcements set to go out at specific intervals, technology can be used by any effective and efficient leader to maintain that high-quality communication style that needs to occur within the life of a congregation to be successful.

Listening as a Form of Communicating

It might seem counterintuitive to hear the statement that listening is a form of effective communication. Earlier in this book, I mentioned the district reconciler who helped a troubled congregation by being an effective and attentive listener to members of the congregation. When I asked him if he could teach me how to do that, he simply answered no. He went on to remind me that listening as a form of communication was a very specific art that many people have a difficult time perfecting.

One reason that listening is hard for many people is because of our desire to either contribute or respond to that which is said to us on a timely basis. I am guilty of this oftentimes as well when people talk to me. My first inclination is to either solve their problem, fix their circumstance, or contribute to what they are saying, rather than simply listen as a form of communication. Good listeners will simply communicate by their attentiveness in listening to that which is being said to them. Effective communicators will listen closely to what is said and create trust by being attentive and genuine.

Throughout my career, I have learned that in circumstances where people come to me with significant anger or frustration, the less I talk, the more I say. Being an effective listener, especially with angry people, can be the difference between being able to provide pastoral care or simply shutting them off altogether. Jesus demonstrates this clear point throughout His ministry. He is patient and compassionate in the interchanges with His disciple Peter, and He listens clearly to the requests and supplications that people make to Him. This is especially true when people who are blind request sight, people who are lame desire to walk, people who are hungry plead for food, and the loved ones of the deceased cry aloud for the power that comes only from the Lord God Himself. Jesus directly responds to the requests that are given to Him, especially in times of need.

Another key aspect of listening as a form of communication comes in listening to the feedback that we receive from the information that we give. I have noticed over time that we have adjusted and changed the way we communicate, and the content of those communications, based on feedback that people have given us from previous communications. Sometimes criticism is not always a bad thing. I know many who call constructive criticism acceptable criticism. For me, there's value in almost every criticism, including criticism about communication. Even dealing with heavy criticism will allow you as an effective communicator to learn what others are having success doing and, in some way, attempt to duplicate that in your own style and method.

Listening takes an effort that many people are not willing to put into communicating. It has been a struggle for me at times in my ministry and my life. However, the older I get the more important I see that listening has become in my ministry and my leadership. Allowing people to communicate and share their thoughts is an effective way to show compassion and care to those you serve. It's also hard to come to grips with this truth, but sometimes it's okay to be silent rather than to talk. This is the one reality that has been so surprising to me throughout my recent career as bishop and president. Simply taking the time to listen and understand what people are trying to communicate as a form of care has been a significant part of my maturation process. I have learned clearly that listening to others affirms the speaker and the communicator and allows for a deeper connection and a broader form of trust to be built.

Conclusion

There is no doubt in my mind that effective and clear communication from the leadership position is critical and crucial for success within the ministry. Unfortunately, too often I have seen pastors who do not care about effective or efficient communication. They find themselves stuck in some archaic, old-fashioned way of writing a monthly newsletter, thereby alienating many people who could benefit from more frequent and more concise communication on a regular basis. On the other hand, throughout my career, I have had laymen and women who have asked me for a monthly newsletter as I began the weekly updates and over time found themselves converted to appreciating regular and frequent communication versus a monthly newsletter with a specific article written by the pastor. Regardless of whether you utilize weekly or monthly communication, be consistent and direct in the information you are sharing. Don't waste people's time with gobbledygook and nonsense that they cannot use in their life.

Practice being clear and concise in your regular communication rather than verbose and long-winded. People will appreciate the pointedness in your communication and the respect that you have for the time that they take to read what you are writing or listen to what you are saying. Clarity and conciseness are two values that affect them, which leaders must conquer in order to achieve longevity and connectivity. Being able to effectively communicate the things you are trying to share with your people will become the difference between success and failure as a pastoral leader. Making a connection with your people by communicating with them is likewise a very important activity that every pastoral leader should focus on.

Understanding and compassion are hallmarks of the Office of the Holy Ministry and anyone who fulfills that office. Ensuring that all communication is had with understanding and compassion is an important skill set for an effective pastoral leader seeking to be a communicator. The Office of the Holy Ministry is an office of communication, whether in preaching, teaching, or simply writing a newsletter or email. Everything the Office of the Holy Ministry does is about communication.

Using the technique of repetition to communicate will be an important tool for any effective pastoral leader. Understanding the reality that repetition creates remembrance allows for the pastoral leader to focus on helping his people to retain that which he is trying to communicate. Repetition used properly is a help, not a hindrance to leadership, and it moves you toward being an effective communicator to the people you serve. Using repetition in a negative way can also be a negative element of your leadership style with the people that you serve. Use repetition in a positive way to help solidify the information and knowledge that you are trying to communicate.

Since the pastoral office is a teaching office, you should invest in helping others become effective and efficient in their communication skills as well. Leaders within the congregation who are good communicators can only help the ministry. Leaders who are poor in their communication style can do nothing but damage the work of the church, even if that's not their desire. I have been a party to a number of situations as the bishop and president of the English District where well-meaning congregational leaders have been poor communicators, and this has triggered conflict within the congregation that was simply unnecessary and unwarranted. Help others be successful in their communication skills as you work to be an effective communicator yourself.

Remember to overcommunicate the information you are seeking to transmit as a form of transparency. The goal of clear and concise communication is to transfer the information needed by the hearer. Whether you are giving updates to the schedule, location, and time of events or announcing the death of a loved one in the church, communicating with the people of God in your parish is a critical element to making sure that people are updated and feel connected to the work that the church is doing. Overcommunicating sometimes is necessary to get the message across and help people retain the information you are communicating.

Finally, be a listener. Demonstrate love and care for your people by listening to what they say and digesting their feedback from your communication as a means to becoming a more effective communicator. Listen before you speak as a demonstration of care and love for the people you serve. Trust that the Holy Spirit will use you according to His will and His way to communicate those things He is desiring for the sake of His people.

REFLECTIONS

1. Do you struggle to communicate effectively and efficiently with others?
2. Is listening as a form of communication difficult for you?
3. List five ways that you can be more effective in your communication strategy with others.
4. Discuss times and ways in which others have struggled in their communication with you.
5. What are some clear biblical examples of positive communication?
6. Using repetition in your communication style to be effective and efficient without becoming irritating and off-putting can be difficult. Discuss ways of being repetitious and concise at the same time.
7. How does helping others in their communication help you in your role of leadership within the congregation or ministerial setting?

CHAPTER VIII

Uplifting Others to Lead: Servant Leadership

One marker for determining leadership success is how well those who are underneath you lead themselves and those under their care. Empowering those throughout the congregation and ministry to lead in their capacities is a quality and a trait of any successful pastoral leader, and will only contribute to the overall success and well-being of the church or the ministry where you serve. Too often, I have worked with very good theologians who have trouble with others being successful to those leaders underneath them. I have always taken the approach that the better those who serve with me are in their aspects of leadership, the better I am as a leader myself. Having a team mentality that focuses on the success of all on the team, rather than simply on the captain of the team, will always drive the team toward success and stability.

The best leaders that I have had the pleasure to learn from were those who uplifted me and helped me to be the best leader I could be. Shortly after graduating from Concordia Theological Seminary in Fort Wayne, Indiana, I was ordained and installed by Rev. Dr. David Ritt, president of the English District. He was very kind to me at the time and still to this very day has remained a significant influence on my leadership style and success. Early on in my career, he appointed me a circuit visitor when there was a vacancy in our circuit in Pittsburgh. I had not yet turned thirty years old when this appointment was given to me. I remember the call to this very day; he began by telling me that he was appointing me a circuit visitor. He knew that I had the capacity and the ability to carry out the responsibilities of the office. Throughout my tenure as a circuit visitor, he was always gracious and uplifting in helping me be successful. His regular encouragement, as well as his occasional brotherly correction, kept me focused and passionate to do the best that I could do.

This is just one example of many in my life where those I served under took the time to invest in me as a leader and uplift me in my role toward supporting the overall work of the Church and the organization that we were serving. From the very beginning of my service in the Church, I was shown servant leadership by those leaders who uplifted me and others in subordinate leadership positions to help make everyone a better team in service to Christ and the Church. True servant leadership will always seek to better those you are leading in order to help subordinates be successful and effective in their current roles.

Another key factor to being a successful servant leader while uplifting others in their leadership position is not being intimidated when those who are underneath you have success. Throughout my career, I have been blessed with leaders who have not suppressed my advancement, but instead assisted in any way possible to help me move forward in my leadership role and position me to utilize the gifts that God has given to me. The sinful side of any person can lead them to suppress high-quality leaders serving underneath him in order to retain some form of control. I have made it my habit as bishop and president of the English District to try to provide an opportunity for those within the church to be able to utilize their God-given gifts in leadership. This is especially true with some of our younger pastors who have come out of the seminary. I have tried very hard to intentionally work to provide opportunities for potential young leaders to be given roles and responsibilities to flourish and succeed.

Invest in the Young Leader

As I have said previously, several leaders in my life saw potential in me and invested time and energy from my early days at college until this very day. I could take up several pages talking about the men in my life who have so graciously invested time and energy in me as a leader. It is humbling when I sit down and spend time contemplating all the contributors in my life who have supported me, uplifted me, and consistently encouraged me to use the gifts that God has given me to be the best leader that I can be. Unfortunately, that has not always been the case in every instance or at every time in my career. I have met moments of great resistance regarding my leadership, especially early on in my ministry and career. When those moments have occurred in my life, I have always remembered 1 Timothy 4:6–16:

> If you put these things before the brothers, you will be a good servant of Christ Jesus, being trained in the words of the faith and of the good doctrine that you have followed. Have nothing to do with irreverent, silly myths. Rather train yourself for godliness; for while bodily training is of some value, godliness is of value in every way, as it holds promise for the present life and also for the life to come. The saying is trustworthy and deserving of full acceptance. For to this end we toil and strive, because we have our hope set on the living God, who is the Savior of all people, especially of those who believe.
>
> Command and teach these things. *Let no one despise you for your youth, but set the believers an example in speech, in conduct, in love, in faith, in purity* [emphasis mine]. Until I come, devote yourself to the public reading of Scripture, to exhortation, to teaching. Do not neglect the gift you have, which was given you by prophecy when the council of elders laid their hands on you. Practice these things, immerse yourself in them, so that all may see your progress. Keep a close watch on yourself and on the teaching. Persist in this, for by so doing you will save both yourself and your hearers.

This passage has been one that has become a very important part of my understanding of leadership and the encouragement to uplift others in leadership. Especially 1 Timothy 4:12, "Let no one despise you for your youth, but set the believers an example in speech, in conduct, in love, in faith, in purity." As I grow older, this passage has become one of the foundational passages that remind me of the importance of not treating young leaders with disdain or disrespect. Throughout my career, it has always been the older pastoral leaders who understood this passage who treated me with respect and provided me with opportunities for growth in my life as a pastoral leader.

Whenever I am dealing with a young leader in the church, I am always reminded of 1 Timothy 4:12 and the importance of respecting the gifts that God has given to all men at every age. It is so easy as an older man to simply dismiss a youthful leader and to allow life experience to overtake youthfulness and passion. The 1 Timothy text does not just talk about respecting the youthful leader; it also reminds us to continue to devote ourselves to the public reading of Scripture, to exhortation, and to the teachings of the Bible. As I grow older, I have found this to be especially important for me as a leader to remember and to inwardly digest. Being a leader in the church and speaking the truth in love will oftentimes lead to someone having hard feelings. Making sure that all you do is centered around and connected to the public reading of the Word of God and His teachings will help to minimize this reality.

It becomes very easy to lose focus as a leader when you are tempted to protect your position rather than uplift others in their leadership roles. The Timothy text quoted above also goes on to remind us in verses 14–16, "Do not neglect the gift you have, which was given you by prophecy when the council of elders laid their hands on you. Practice these things, immerse yourself in them, so that all may see your progress. Keep a close watch on yourself and on the teaching. Persist in this, for by so doing you will save both yourself and your hearers."

We should not forget the gifts that God has provided to us in the role of pastoral leadership. It is crucial for any good pastoral leader to persist in the public teaching of God's Word, in the proper administration of the Sacraments of the Church, and in the faithful witness toward Christ and the Church until He returns. The greatest example of leadership in this vein is our own Lord and Savior, Jesus Christ. He maintained and persisted in the work of salvation even to the point of death. When Jesus was tempted in the wilderness with the three great temptations from Satan, He met each temptation with a biblical foundational principle and trust in the Old Testament declarations.

Jesus understood that diversity of experience in His disciple pool was important. He called hardworking fishermen, tax collectors, family men, and doubters as His disciples and future leaders. It is clearly evident that He understood the importance of having disciples with a variety of ages and experience levels. Jesus invested in His disciples at various different ages and stages. His desire for servant leadership is clearly articulated throughout the entirety of His teachings and in His reflection on Old Testament characters.

Each disciple that Jesus chose had specific and unique gifts that came directly from the Holy Spirit. While Jesus firmly and completely ascribed to uplifting all leaders, even those who were younger, He filled His disciple pool with men dedicated to the work of the Church in the ministry of the Gospel. There is no doubt in my mind that Jesus understood the principle of getting the right people in the right positions at the right time. Jim Collins, in his book *Good to Great,* makes this point very clear and precise. Effective leaders must equip those leaders around them with the skill sets necessary to be effective and efficient. This is especially true with young leaders in the Bible, as well as Jesus Himself.

You Don't Need a Title to Be a Leader

Mark Sanborn is credited with coining the phrase "You don't need a title to be a leader." Throughout my dissertation study, I found no greater phrase that describes the importance of uplifting others than this one. The concept seems simple, but it is actually very hard to understand and even more difficult to implement. The idea that a person doesn't need to have a title in order to lead is a logical concept yet simultaneously confusing. For most people, thinking about leadership immediately invokes an understanding of the station or position of the person who is leading. Throughout history, the most successful people have always garnered great titles and positions as they left their imprint and legacy in the leadership roles that they had. Whether discussing presidents of countries, chief executive officers of corporations, coaches of professional athletic teams, or individual athletes, we always remember the great titles and positions that people have. But in fact, some of the greatest contributions to leadership are done by people who have no titles.

Throughout my career, the greatest contributions made to the ministries and congregations I have served were done by title-less laymen and women, people of God who had a passion for serving others and loving their neighbor. Servants of the Church who carried out their passion and faith in the form of service and dedication to the mission and ministry in front of them. Whether we're discussing the husband and wife who quietly cut the grass every week at church, the mother and daughter who weekly prepare the Lord's altar with the bread and wine used in the Divine Service, or the single man who dedicates his life to cleaning the church and maintaining the building, we see people of God who love the Lord and have no titles being leaders.

One of the points that I share with new seminarians coming to congregations in my district is clearly to never ignore those in the congregation who don't have leadership positions. There is no doubt in my mind that some of the greatest contributions in congregational ministry come at the hands of title-less leaders. These are the people of God who simply put forth an effort to do the jobs within the ministry and the congregation that need to be done without a title, or in some cases without even being asked. This is one area where I believe young pastors can learn a great deal in the development of their leadership style. Pastors indeed have significant influence in the ministry and congregation where they serve. That influence should be utilized to uplift and encourage people to serve God in the church even if they do not have a title or a role of prominence.

Some of the greatest contributions in the New Testament came from people who had no title and yet performed a significant function in biblical history and theological context. One of those biblical characters that comes to mind is Simon of Cyrene. Here you have a man who played a very small but significant role in the Passion of Jesus Christ. After enduring excruciating beatings, mocking, and trials, Jesus was at His physical limitation as He carried His cross to Golgotha for the crescendo of the messianic life. Exhaustion set in, and His body gave way. Simon, who was simply in town witnessing the event, was called upon to participate in the Savior's final steps toward His crucifixion. Never named before and never named again in Scripture, Simon did not have a title other than a helper in carrying the cross of Jesus.

Another title-less leader who played a significant theological role and yet had no great title was the woman at the well—in fact, the Bible never even names her. The Gospel of John 4:7–26 reminds us,

> A woman from Samaria came to draw water. Jesus said to her, "Give Me a drink." (For His disciples had gone away into the city to buy food.) The Samaritan woman said to Him, "How is it that You, a Jew, ask for a drink from me, a woman of Samaria?" (For Jews have no dealings with Samaritans.) Jesus answered her, "If you knew the gift of God, and who it is that is saying to you, 'Give Me a drink,' you would have asked Him, and He would have given you living water." The woman said to him, "Sir, You have nothing to draw water with, and the well is deep. Where do You get that living water? Are You greater than our father Jacob? He gave us the well and drank from it himself, as did his sons and his livestock." Jesus said to her, "Everyone who drinks of this water will be thirsty again, but whoever drinks of the water that I will give him will never be thirsty again. The water that I will give him will become in him a spring of water welling up to eternal life." The woman said to Him, "Sir, give me this water, so that I will not be thirsty or have to come here to draw water."

> Jesus said to her, "Go, call your husband, and come here." The woman answered Him, "I have no husband." Jesus said to her, "You are right in saying, 'I have no husband'; for you have had five husbands, and the one you now have is not your husband. What you have said is true." The woman said to Him, "Sir, I perceive that You are a prophet. Our fathers worshiped on this mountain, but You say that in Jerusalem is the place where people ought to worship." Jesus said to her, "Woman, believe Me, the hour is coming when neither on this mountain nor in Jerusalem will you worship the Father. You worship what you do not know; we worship what we know, for salvation is from the Jews. But the hour is coming, and is now here, when the true worshipers will worship the Father in spirit and truth, for the Father is seeking such people to worship Him. God is spirit, and those who worship Him must worship in spirit and truth." The woman said to Him, "I know that Messiah is coming (He who is called Christ). When He comes, He will tell us all things." Jesus said to her, "I who speak to you am He."

The interchange between Jesus and the woman at the well is one of the most significant theological interchanges of the New Testament. Jesus tells the sinful woman that He is the living water and that He can do the great things of health, healing, and forgiveness. This interchange sets the stage for Jesus to declare His messianic role. There are other significant points in this biblical text as well, including the fact that this conversation took place between Jesus (a Jew) and a Samaritan woman. It demonstrates the importance of investing in people regardless of the title that they have—or even if they have no title at all. Jesus takes a servant woman and throughout a conversation both teaches and professes His mercy, love, and grace to the nameless woman and the world.

Another significant leadership example in the Bible is the story of the Good Samaritan from Luke 10:25–37:

> And behold, a lawyer stood up to put Him to the test, saying, "Teacher, what shall I do to inherit eternal life?" He said to him, "What is written in the Law? How do you read it?" And he answered, "You shall love the Lord your God with all your heart and with all your soul and with all your strength and with all your mind, and your neighbor as yourself." And He said to him, "You have answered correctly; do this, and you will live."
>
> But he, desiring to justify himself, said to Jesus, "And who is my neighbor?" Jesus replied, "A man was going down from Jerusalem to Jericho, and he fell among robbers, who stripped him and beat him and departed, leaving him half dead. Now by chance a priest was going down that road, and when he saw him he passed by on the other side. So likewise a Levite, when he came to the place and saw him, passed by on the other side. But a Samaritan, as he journeyed, came to where he was, and when he saw him, he had compassion. He went to him and bound up his wounds, pouring on oil and wine. Then he set him on his own animal and brought him to an inn and took care of him. And the next day he took out two denarii and gave them to the innkeeper, saying, 'Take care of him, and whatever more you spend, I will repay you when I come back.' Which of these three, do you think, proved to be a neighbor to the man who fell among the robbers?" He said, "The one who showed him mercy." And Jesus said to him, "You go, and do likewise."

Here we have another example of a title-less leader who was carrying out the functions of leadership that the priest and the rabbi should have been doing as they passed by the stranger. In this case, a man, not named except to say he was a Samaritan, bound up the wounds of the beaten man, took him to the inn, and paid for his care. There was no title for the Samaritan man, there was no great position that he had that garnered attention. He simply had compassion and mercy on the man in need. Jesus declares to the lawyer, "You go, and do likewise" (v. 37). Every title-less leader I have ever dealt with has the Samaritan heart of simply doing what is necessary to care for and love their neighbor, not seeking credit or accolades.

Say Thanks and Show Appreciation

While it might seem normal or seem like it should go without saying, many pastors forget the importance of simply saying thank you for the service provided to God in the church. Oftentimes within the church, many things are accomplished by very few members. In fact, throughout my career every congregation and every ministry I have been a part of has always had a nuclear core of people who performed important functions and difficult jobs without even being asked. It is very tempting for the leader to be appreciative of those accomplishing the tasks but never recognize them for their participation and contribution.

A wise leader once told me that simply saying thanks and recognizing the contributions that people make privately or publicly will go a long way to uplifting and encouraging those within the congregation who are leaders in the ministry. This concept and practice have become very important to me in my role as bishop and president. I try as often as I can to highlight the district staff as well as the church workers and lay leaders of the congregations throughout the English District. In my opinion, you can never thank people enough for the dedication and sacrifice they make as title-less leaders in congregations and ministries throughout the church. Any well-run congregation or ministry has a host of people who are never asked and simply do. These people ought to be recognized and thanked for their contribution and effort.

I try very hard to personally thank people for the contributions they make and the participation they have within the church and the ministry. As sinful human people, we can forget and drop the ball on this very simple practice as leaders in the church and in ministry. I have found throughout my career that I simply need to take responsibility when that happens and ask for forgiveness, and then give thanks for the ministry and work that the people of God are doing. Establishing a culture of thankfulness and appreciation for church workers, lay volunteers, and contributing members is not only wise but also called for by our Lord.

These are some passages that emphasize the importance of giving thanks and taking the time to pray for those in service, thank God for their work, and thank them for taking the time (emphases are mine).

- 1 Thessalonians 5:16–18, "Rejoice always, pray without ceasing, *give thanks in all circumstances*; for this is the will of God in Christ Jesus for you."
- Colossians 2:6–7, "Therefore, as you received Christ Jesus the Lord, so walk in Him, rooted and built up in Him and established in the faith, just as you were taught, *abounding in thanksgiving*."
- Philippians 4:4–7, "Rejoice in the Lord always; again I will say, rejoice. Let your reasonableness be known to everyone. The Lord is at hand; do not be anxious about anything, but in everything by prayer and supplication *with thanksgiving* let your requests be made known to God. And the peace of God, which surpasses all understanding, will guard your hearts and your minds in Christ Jesus."
- 2 Corinthians 9:15, "*Thanks be to God* for His inexpressible gift!"
- 1 Corinthians 1:2–9, "To the church of God that is in Corinth, to those sanctified in Christ Jesus, called to be saints together with all those who in every place call upon the name of our Lord Jesus Christ, both their Lord and ours: Grace to you and peace from God our Father and the Lord Jesus Christ. *I give thanks to my God always for you* because of the grace of God that was given you in Christ Jesus, that in every way you were enriched in Him in all speech and all knowledge—even as the testimony about Christ was confirmed among you—so that you are not lacking in any gift, as you wait for the revealing of our Lord Jesus Christ, who will sustain you to the end, guiltless in the day of our Lord

> Jesus Christ. God is faithful, by whom you were called into the fellowship of His Son, Jesus Christ our Lord."

As we can see, several biblical passages can help us to understand the importance of giving thanks and calling on our God for His blessings and mercy. This is especially true for those who seek to serve Him and do His will. Giving thanks to people is a significant part of helping people become servant leaders in their given and chosen areas. Saying thank you and showing appreciation for the effort is a crucial step in uplifting others in their leadership roles. Creating a culture of thankfulness both to God and to those who serve is the biblical right thing to do.

Spend Time Looking for Future Leaders

One day in my sixth-grade religion class, my pastor simply said to me that I would be a pastor one day. Quickly after Pastor Fisher told me I was going to be a pastor myself, I replied that I was going to play football for the Detroit Lions. Given the performance of my beloved Lions over the last thirty years, I believe I made the right career choice to follow my pastor's exhortation to go into the ministry. I have often told the story of this event to people with a chuckle. But this is the point that I want to make: the greatest way to encourage young people to consider the vocation of a pastoral leader is to identify and actively encourage young men for the Office of the Ministry.

While my pastor was the first to identify and encourage me to go into the office of pastor, I had other laypeople after my pastor who encouraged me to take up the mantle as well and supported me in preparing to serve as a pastor in The Lutheran Church—Missouri Synod. In fact, as a young man, I did not know it but there was a person in my congregation who had already begun to set aside money and send it to the seminary in my name. I had no clue when I enrolled at Concordia Theological Seminary in Fort Wayne that this person had already established a small amount of money in an account in my name to help pay for seminary. It wasn't until his death that I was told that my pastor had put his own money where his mouth was. Not only did he encourage me to go to the seminary to be a pastor but he also provided financial resources for it.

I have been blessed up to this point in my ministry with having six men complete the seminary directly from my parish or the ministries that I have served. It is my personal goal to have twenty-five men go to the ministry from a direct parish or institution that I serve. As a pastoral leader, I encourage all my brother pastors to seek and identify young men and second-career men in their congregation who would be good candidates for the pastoral office. Throughout my time as a district president, I have seen the great influence that one pastor can have on men considering the Office of the Public Ministry.

As I have traveled throughout the English District to all the parishes, I have had the pleasure of meeting especially younger boys where it was evident that the Holy Spirit was resting on them and that their future involved serving God in the Church. As a parish pastor, I take great responsibility and proclaim the Gospel, sharing the love of Christ, forgiving the sins of the penitent, and encouraging others to go into the service of God in the Church. My introduction to considering the pastoral office by my own parish pastor Ralph Fisher remains to this day one of the most impactful conversations and invitations I have ever had, and I strive to have similar conversations with others who may be called into the ministry.

The biblical standard on this topic is very clear, especially from Matthew 9:35–38:

> And Jesus went throughout all the cities and villages, teaching in their synagogues and proclaiming the gospel of the kingdom and healing every disease and every affliction. When He saw the crowds, He had compassion for them, because they were harassed and helpless, like sheep without a shepherd. Then He said to His disciples, "The harvest is plentiful, but the laborers are few; therefore pray earnestly to the Lord of the harvest to send out laborers into His harvest."

Jesus did not just pray; He actively invited many people, saying, "Follow Me." It is important for us not only to pray to God to send laborers into the harvest field but also to personally invite men to consider serving God as pastors and other called workers in the Church, and women to serve as deaconesses, as teachers, and in visitation ministries. It is vitally important for any good leader to continually pray that God would provide others to fulfill the office of leadership in the church as pastors and teachers of the Gospel. Just as my pastor invited me to consider the ministry, good effective pastoral leaders should always be on the lookout for those who fit the profile and have the desire to go into the harvest field to proclaim the Gospel of Jesus Christ to a fallen world.

Having a Bench of Leaders

It has been my experience as bishop and president of the English District of The Lutheran Church—Missouri Synod that many congregations do not have a deep bench when it comes to lay leadership. Oftentimes, congregations simply recycle high-quality lay leaders in different positions throughout the church year after year. There is little to no intentionality to raise up leaders for future service to God in the church. It is very important for good pastoral leaders to consistently build a bench of current and future leaders for the church who understand the mission, the goal, and the importance of biblical fidelity.

Early on in my career, I was having a conversation with the president of my congregation, and a young man within the congregation came up as a potential future leader. We both agreed that this young man would be fantastic for future leadership in the church as president of the congregation. Each of us individually went and spoke to this brother and asked him if he would serve in the leadership role that was needed at that time. This was all with the understanding that down the road this young man would fulfill the office of president as he learned the operations of the church and the culture that had developed in this specific parish.

This was one of the most important activities that I could have done outside of the Divine Service on Sunday morning. Helping to identify and raise up leaders within the church is also a responsibility of the pastoral leader as he builds a deep bench of those who can serve when others have run their course of leadership and service to God in the church. Maintaining a culture of building a bench within a congregation should be always at the forefront of any good pastoral leader.

Conclusion

Simply put, uplift those under your leadership to be successful and flourish. Always remember the principle that when one succeeds, the whole team succeeds. Being an effective leader will allow you to help others be successful within their sphere of leadership. Intentionally uplifting others and placing them in situations where they can be successful is the mark of a true team builder and a leader who has confidence in what the people of his congregation or ministry are doing. Always look forward and do not worry about the success those underneath you are having. They will ultimately be a positive reflection on your leadership and contribute to the success of the overall ministry.

Empowering young leaders within the church and the Christian community is a principle that must be prioritized more. The New Testament is very clear that God gives gifts to people for specific times and places; it's incumbent upon a good effective leader to help especially young potential leaders grow into the skill sets God has provided. Never be afraid to uplift a young leader in your life and ministry out of fear that he may supersede you and be more effective than you. Only pray that God would make that so and that those serving underneath you would become even better leaders than you.

Positions and titles are fun to have, and to some people are the ultimate in their career and life. But the reality is simple: most of the greatest contributions in the life of the church have been accomplished by title-less leaders. Never underestimate or undervalue the leaders in the church who have no title. These people can be some of the most significant and hard-working men and women within the church. In some cases, these are the very engine power that can move the church's life and make it go. Raise the title-less leaders in your congregation as people of God, and value them in the ministry and mission of the congregation.

Don't allow yourself as a leader to take for granted those who serve the church and the mission. Simply recognizing people and showing your appreciation is critical to being an effective leader. Never take people in the church for granted, and always remember their desire and passion to serve God in the church is equal to yours. Being an effective pastoral leader will always be strengthened when you simply thank people for what they do within the church. You can never thank people too much for their dedication to God, the Church, and the mission of the Gospel.

Always be on the lookout and seek those upon whom the Spirit rests to serve the church. Be intentional as a pastoral leader to identify especially young men who may be able to be effective pastoral leaders. Always be ready to encourage anyone who shows interest and the ability to be a servant within the church. I have one beloved brother in my life whom I have continually encouraged to go to the seminary and be a pastor. I will not stop encouraging this man to do this and to serve God as a called and ordained servant of the Word until it is accomplished, or until I am serving the Lord in heaven.

REFLECTIONS

1. Why is it difficult for certain pastoral leaders to uplift others within the congregation and help them to be successful?

2. What can you do to help uplift and encourage leaders within the church to be successful in their given roles?

3. Discuss how empowering young leaders in the church has been beneficial. What are some strategies for uplifting young leaders in your congregation?

4. Have you thanked a church worker or a church leader recently?

5. Do you take for granted those who serve in the church but have no title or position?

6. How can you help establish a culture of thanksgiving in your congregation for those who serve the church?

7. Discuss the biblical passages above regarding a thankful spirit and think of ways that this can be extended within your congregation.

8. Are you an encourager of young men especially to become pastors?

9. How can you or your congregation be more intentional in encouraging and uplifting especially young people to service and careers in church work?

CHAPTER IX

Financial Matters and Why They Are Important

The financial situation of congregations and nonprofit ministries is very important and is a topic that does not garner enough attention in leadership. I did not always think that was the case; I only fell in love with finances after I was in my career. Before that, I would hear conversations about budgeting and finance talk within the council and the voters assembly at my congregation.

One day at a voters meeting, a beloved member of my congregation stood up and declared a simple phrase that has never left me. He said, "No money, no mission." This phrase at the time was somewhat offensive to me and caused me frustration as I responded to him with, "Where is your trust in God?" As I matured in pastoral leadership and personal growth, I realized that the saying he put forth at the meeting is true.

The saying "No money, no mission" is also, in many respects, a very biblical understanding. The parable of the talents in the Gospel of Matthew reminds us that God does not bless those who bury their talents or money. Instead, He rewards those who are good stewards and blesses their work abundantly. Ever since that time, I have enjoyed the topic of finances and administration within the church.

I know for many conservative theologians this topic will raise the hair on the back of their necks. I have had way too many pastors tell me throughout my career that I don't need to know about finances; I'll have laymen and women to help me with that.

I have had other pastors say the finances of the congregation are for the laity, not for the pastoral office. I've had yet other pastors tell me I am called to teach, to preach, and to visit; managing finances is not a part of my call. All these positions show a lack of understanding when it comes to sound biblical stewardship and congregational health and wellness. The most effective pastoral leaders I know are also good fiscal stewards as the leaders within their congregations.

I will make the assertion here as I have many times in my career as a district president and bishop: pastors who take the approach that financial matters are not a part of pastoral leadership fail in their role as a leader. I realize this is a very strong assertion and for some can be offensive. However, I believe the biblical model is very clear—pastors must know what is happening with the ministries that God has entrusted to them physically as well as financially. To take the approach that the only responsibility that the pastor has is spiritual in nature is to ignore the call from God to lead His people in all aspects of congregational life and ministry.

During my career as a district president, I have seen too many cases where pastors have handed over the financial reins to the laity without giving any input or supervision, and in 100 percent of those cases I have seen nothing but disasters occur. That is not to say that the laymen and women who have been entrusted with these financial matters are incompetent. In fact, in many cases the laity I have worked with are very educated and dedicated servants. The conflict arises when the pastor has ignored the financial conditions of the congregation, and difficult situations quickly arise that had been building over time. Unfortunately, this is generally the time that the district president and bishop is called into a conversation, long after things could have been done to prevent the financial condition that the congregation has found themselves in.

It is not simply enough to teach good biblical stewardship from the pastoral office. Effective leaders must also model biblical stewardship in their own personal lives and as the spiritual head of the congregation. Ignoring or delegating this responsibility to someone else is always a recipe for disaster and conflict within the life of the parish. I am not saying that a pastor has to be an expert, nor am I saying that a pastor must be the one who deals with the finances. I am simply asserting that a pastor must have a basic and working knowledge of the finances of the congregation and how the financial health of the congregation is progressing.

Finance Terms Every Pastor Should Know

What follows is a list of financial terms and definitions in alphabetical order that every pastoral leader ought to at least be familiar with as he carries out his duties within the congregation and ministry to which he has been called. During my doctoral studies, I was exposed to the Harvard Business School Online, which has a plethora of helpful insights and very good, easily understandable financial pieces. These terms are just some of the key and important terms that you ought to be aware of as you carry out your function as a leader.

Assets: Assets are items your congregation owns that can provide future benefits to ministry, such as cash, inventory, real estate, office equipment, or accounts receivable. There are different types of assets, including the following:

Current Assets: These might include money market accounts, stocks, or other liquid forms of congregational assets that can be turned into cash within a year.

Fixed Assets: These are funds that a congregation owns but can't immediately turn into cash, such as mutual funds and long-term fixed-return investments. These generate long-term income for congregations and ministries, which often use them as an endowment where assets are placed and used to generate future income.

Asset Allocation: Most of the congregations that I have in my district do not have to be concerned with asset allocation. But for congregations and ministries with investments or an endowment fund, asset allocation is how they choose to distribute their money between different types of investments, or asset classes. This diversification of assets protects long-term funds when particular market sectors decline sharply. These allocations include the following:

Bonds: When your congregation buys a bond, you're essentially lending money, typically to the government or a corporation. The congregation receives interest payments at set intervals and gets back the loaned amount when the bond matures—or after a specified term when the bond can be redeemed.

Cash and Cash Equivalents: This is obviously the congregation's cash reserves, and any asset that can easily be turned into cash when necessary.

Stocks: Some congregations and ministries invest in stocks. A stockholder owns a share of a public or private company. When your congregation buys stock in a company, it becomes a shareholder and can receive a share of the company's profits, called dividends, when they are distributed.

Balance Sheet: This is a financial statement that lists the assets and liabilities of a congregation or organization. It shows the ministry's worth, or "book value." The balance sheet (often referred to as the Treasurer's Report) usually shows a list of assets or income and the total value of those assets at the top. Below that is a listing of liabilities or expenses. The liabilities plus the church's equity should equal the total assets.

Capital Gain: Capital gain measures the difference between the amount your congregation initially paid for an asset or investment (or the value of a donation it received) and its value when sold. An increase in value is called a capital gain; a loss of value is a capital loss. This becomes important if you have excess cash in the congregation and you have investments that generate income or grow. In my congregation, we had two small investments, and regularly the congregation used the income from these two for growth and ministry opportunities.

Cash Flow: This is the amount of the congregation or ministry's cash that is moving in and out at a particular time. Cash flow is a crucial element for any pastor to be aware of as he leads his church. Poor or low cash flow can cause a congregation to struggle mightily with its overall health and wellness because it does not have enough cash on hand to pay bills or salaries. Too often in my ministry, I have come across pastors, as well as church leaders, who cared little or nothing about cash flow. This has always led to difficulty in ministry and constant conflict with the congregations. Maintaining healthy cash flow is one way to manage a congregation well.

Cash Flow Statement: This financial statement shows what happened to a congregation or ministry's cash during a given period (usually a month, a quarter, or a year). This report shows how the congregation received and spent its cash over that period. It includes an overview of operating, investing, and financing activities during the reporting period.

Compound Interest: This is sometimes described as "interest on interest." When your congregation deposits money in an interest-bearing account, interest is earned over time and added to that original amount deposited. This new balance then accumulates interest over time. When this new interest is added, the savings or investment grows that much faster. Compound interest is a great way for congregations and ministries to grow their savings and investments. But the same compound interest can also increase your debt for money you borrow. Compound interest is charged on the initial amount you were loaned, increasing the amount that must be paid as the interest is added to your outstanding balance over time. Compounding interest is one of the greatest financial tools that a congregation or ministry can utilize to grow their net assets over time. This provides for more ability to do ministry and missions throughout the life of the congregation.

Depreciation: Depreciation is the amount an asset's value decreases over time. This could include the value of your church computer, printer, or sound equipment. This is generally reflected in a financial statement when discussing a congregation or ministry's facilities or equipment. It is important to think of depreciation as how much of an asset's value the congregation has used over time. That will help prevent this decreasing value from skewing the financial statements in a way that makes your congregation look far worse off than it may be.

EBITDA: This is an acronym that stands for *Earnings Before Interest, Taxes, Depreciation, and Amortization*, or the total cash that comes into your congregation and ministry through offerings, donations, interest, etc. EBITDA measures your congregation or ministry's ability to generate cash flow to pay bills and salaries. To figure your congregation's EBITDA, you would add net profit, interest, taxes, depreciation, and amortization together. While this is not used by many congregations, it does show the true health and wellness of any congregation or ministry from a financial perspective.

Income Statement: This financial report summarizes a congregation or ministry's income and expenses during a given period. An income statement is sometimes called a profit and loss (P&L) statement. This is one method of financial measurement that all congregations and ministries should be paying attention to regularly to see if their offerings and donations are covering their congregation's expenses. Over my time as the bishop and president of the English District, I have seen way too many situations where congregations had no idea what their income statement even looked like, let alone whether it was healthy or not. As a pastoral leader, know the income statement and where the variations may be as you discuss the financial situation at your ministry or parish.

Liabilities: These are the opposite of assets. Liabilities are debts your ministry owes to others, such as bank debt, wages, and money due to companies that supply your congregational needs, also known as accounts payable. Different types of liabilities include the following:

Current Liabilities: Sometimes called short-term liabilities, these are the bills that are due within the next year.

Long-Term Liabilities: These are financial obligations a congregation or ministry is not likely to be able to pay off in a year, but must be paid off over a longer period, like a mortgage.

Liquidity: This describes how quickly you can convert your congregation's assets into cash. Clearly cash itself is the most liquid asset. Your least liquid assets are items like real estate or land because these can take weeks or months to sell. That is the reason some ministries and congregations may have large assets like buildings and property and still struggle to pay salaries and bills because they lack a cash flow and have a low overall income.

Net Worth: Net worth is the value of your congregation's assets after subtracting what it owes in bills, debt payments, salaries, and other expenses. The remaining number shows you the overall state of your ministry's financial health. This can also help guide the decisions you make in the future pertaining to financial matters.

Return On Investment (ROI): Return On Investment compares the cost of a project or activity with the expected return or value that it will bring to your congregation's ministry. Typically, this number is shown as a percentage. You can use this percentage to evaluate whether a project will be worthwhile for your ministry to pursue. In business, ROI is calculated using the following equation: ROI = [(Income – Cost) / Cost] × 100. That can be difficult for a congregation because the return for projects and activities cannot always be measured in monetary terms. But measuring the cost of a congregational activity compared to the ministry benefits it will bring is important so you know whether activities and projects are worth the time, money, and effort involved. In most cases, this is never a thought for congregations, and they will carry on with activities and fundraisers that have a low or zero ROI for the congregation.

An example of this is the spaghetti dinner that we did at my parish early on. After doing the spaghetti dinner for several years, I decided to calculate how many volunteer hours and how much total volunteer product we received from members and subtracted that from the amount of money we earned in the fundraiser for the preschool. It turned out that we could have simply taken the dollar amounts of the supplies that people donated and given that to the church without any effort, and we would have made more money than we did during the actual fundraising event. After the second year of doing this on a negative ROI, I encouraged the leadership to cease doing this fundraiser and instead simply request financial support. The result was a significant increase in overall income for the preschool.

Valuation: Valuation is the process of determining the current worth of an asset, company, or liability. There are a variety of ways you can value your congregation or ministry, but regularly repeating the process is helpful, because you're then ready if ever faced with opportunities or challenges.

Working Capital: Working capital is the difference between a congregation or ministry's current assets and current liabilities. Working capital—the money available for daily operations—can help determine a church's operational efficiency and short-term financial health and wellness.

Basic Budgeting and How It Should Work

Over my career as a pastor, especially when I first began, budgeting was a mere exercise of examining how much money we spent last year in any given category and possibly adding or subtracting a few dollars based on last year's performance. This is a common technique utilized in many congregations to make an attempt at budgeting for the upcoming programmatic and fiscal year. Unfortunately, it lacks clarity and depth and can lead to significant financial hardship and trouble in the life of the congregation.

The simple question must be asked: What is a budget and how should it be used? A budget is a financial forecast model on how income and expenses will be utilized in the upcoming fiscal year in the life of the ministry or organization. Therefore, budgets ought to be clear, concise, and as accurate as possible. Looking at the needs of the congregation or corporation must not simply be a quick view of what the previous year has been. Detailed information and financial data should be used when analyzing the needs of the congregation or corporation for the upcoming fiscal year.

Historically, congregations that utilize elementary assumptions and financial data tend to find themselves in difficulty throughout the fiscal year. Without examining trends and forecasts of relevant information regarding forecasted inflationary expenses, congregations can find themselves having large, unexpected outlays of cash, especially in areas like energy, travel, and maintenance. One recent example of this reality came in the quarterly reporting of Fortune 500 companies in the spring of 2022. During the quarterly earnings announcement, one company stood out by forecasting the impending implications of gasoline costing five dollars per gallon, which was reflected in their quarterly performance. That company was Home Depot. The executive leadership of Home Depot had budgeted and planned for higher transportation costs and had a more accurate level than their peers. This allowed them to weather that storm as their expense forecasts were much more in line with actuals rather than their peer companies who saw distortions in their expenses budgeted for those areas.

This is just one example to prove the point that accurate forecasting and utilization of financial assumptions in metrics are critically important to make an effective budget for future expenses as well as future income. Simply taking a round number either on the expense side or on the income side to prepare a budget is laziness and can be catastrophic within the ministry. I would urge a more serious look at budgeting within the congregation and the life of the organization. Effective leaders will always remain focused and ahead of the curve when dealing with budgets within their corporation or congregation.

Another significant point to budgeting is potentially having to adjust budgets midyear based on unexpected expenses or a drastic reduction in income. Too often in congregational life, I have witnessed churches and ministries ride out a budget even when that budget had faulty assumptions and misguided market conditions. Unfortunately, churches and corporations must effectively adapt to market conditions that drastically affect income or expenses within any congregational or ministry budget. These would include inflation, higher interest rates, supply chain disruption, inflated energy costs, and job layoffs. All of these combine to have a dramatic effect on congregational finances and giving over time. Ignoring these realities oftentimes can cause great catastrophe within the ministry or the congregation. I have seen too many examples of overly drastic cutting at the end of the fiscal year rather than making small adjustments throughout the fiscal year to allow for success when dealing with budgets.

While theological matters within the congregation are the highest priority for the pastor, financial matters should also be important in the health and wellness of any congregation or ministry. Effective leaders will always pay attention and know where the financial situation is for the ministry that they serve. Never become lazy or complacent when it comes to financial matters within the congregation.

Why should the pastor be involved in the budgeting process? This question varies from congregation to congregation. Some congregations historically have had no input from the pastor regarding the budget or its process, while other congregations rely heavily on the pastor to give suggestions and direction as it pertains to items such as congregational giving, support staff, and overall stewardship. These matters are all spiritual in nature as they seek to help and support the public ministry and proclamation of the Gospel. There is no doubt in my mind that all financial matters are theological matters. Therefore, the pastor ought to be involved in the budget preparation and budget discussions throughout the entirety of the process.

Congregational Investments

One area where congregations struggle to do the right thing from a stewardship perspective is investing excess proceeds or excess cash that they have. This is especially true with older congregations that have had a pattern of behavior that has not changed for quite some time. I have dealt with congregations that have held as much as $200,000 in a general checking account rather than investing that money in CDs or mutual funds. These congregations tend to hoard cash to feel comfortable and secure in the ministry that they are doing. But in fact, hoarding large amounts of cash is negative. The cost of the missed opportunity to invest that money and get a return on that investment is tantamount to burying their talent in the ground, as in Matthew 25:24–30.

So the church must be asked the question, What are they doing with excess cash? In some cases, excess cash can be money given as a memorial for any specific reason or event, profitability after a productive year in operations of the ministry, or estate gifts given after a beloved member passes away. In any case, examining what to do with excess cash is important to the overall stewardship of the congregation as well as its longevity in the ministry areas where they serve. Historically, in the 1970s and '80s, CD rates were quite high because the federal funds rate was high as well. Over the last fifteen to twenty years, the federal funds rate had been in decline. This has only recently been reversed, and interest rates are now on the rise.

The great debate in especially conservative congregations is whether to invest in stocks/mutual funds or certificates of deposit. The ultra-conservative church member will always lean toward certificates of deposit because of the protections with FDIC insurance and the guaranteed return. However, when doing a deep dive and analyzing the return on any given mutual fund versus the paltry 1.25 percent that many CDs are paying over the last three to five years, it is important for congregations to make prayerful yet informed decisions on all financial matters.

The next question that must be asked is this: Does the congregation have an endowment fund? If the answer to this question is no, immediately you know one of the tasks before you as a leader is to work on the establishment of a congregational endowment. An endowment can generate future income with current contributions. By employing a strategic asset usage policy, congregations can build an endowment that perpetually will grow as it funds immediate ministerial work and missions. One way that congregational endowment funds can be set up is with a spending policy of only profits raised within the specific endowment portfolio. When the fund has a positive net performance, a funding model automatically is set in motion whereby 75 percent of the profits and proceeds from the growth are used for ministry and mission, while the remaining 25 percent is kept in the fund for perpetual and future growth through compound interest.

The theory behind any well-run endowment is to continually grow the fund while immediately generating income and support for the missions and ministry of the congregation. Too often in congregations today, laity refuse to understand the compounding interest principles that are utilized when spending 75 percent of the generated profits. This ongoing and perpetual income stream is utilized to fund missions and ministry when general congregation offerings are in decline or are withheld altogether. Undoubtedly, congregations must look to the future ministry and mission opportunities in the congregation as they prepare to fund the work of the church. The funding of the ministry is a legacy of faith and a dedication to serving our neighbors. Missional congregations that have significant financial resources understand the delicate balance of maintaining a large robust membership list versus adhering to a clear theological understanding of the Scriptures and the Confessions.

Decision-Making regarding Budget

Another area where I find conflict in congregations revolving around the budget process is in trustee or maintenance decisions and knowing who is responsible for making those decisions. In my direct experience, congregations that do not have a clearly defined process on how and what to fix regarding the facility and the main congregational sanctuary will always find themselves in a conflict situation. When there is a vacuum of process, procedure, or leadership, inevitably what occurs is someone steps in to take on the task of leadership. That does not mean that the person who stepped up is always the right person for the job. I have learned over the course of my leadership time that when there is a lack of leadership the person who generally steps up is not the right person for the job from the beginning. Likewise, often I have seen people step up where there is a lack of leadership out of frustration or guilt, leading to a term of service motivated by frustration and anger.

It is my firm belief and experience that pastors must be tied into and attuned with what is going on within the congregation in every aspect. The pastor ought not to be the lead on trustee or maintenance issues; however, he'd better be fully and completely aware of the needs and what is being done to meet those needs. It will be expected of any pastoral leader that he has a grasp on and knowledge about matters that pertain to the congregation, especially those that deal with the facility and the physical property. Once again, I do not recommend that any pastoral leader take the overall lead in these building or maintenance issues. He must be tied into and knowledgeable about these matters. He also has the unique ability to help generate volunteers and support for those who are physically doing these things around the congregation in ministry.

Another area where I believe pastors must step up and become more engaged and invested is the negotiation process, in which every ministry or congregation engages him. Pastoral leaders should be able to make the case in every and all circumstances where the congregation can be given a good deal or a financial break. Good negotiators understand that the process of negotiation is a dance and has a rhythm to it. All the high-quality leaders I have been trained under or have watched have helped to imprint on me the importance of being an effective and knowledgeable negotiator.

One of the biggest mistakes that pastors make when dealing with decision-making around budgets is trying to control the situation rather than participate in it. It is much easier for the leader to simply control the situation rather than let others on the council or the board of elders participate in it as budget decisions are made. One of my pet peeves, and one of my historic problems as bishop and president of the English District, is when pastors are totally and completely not a part of the decision-making process when it comes to budgeting in the congregation. On the other hand, I have had many difficult situations where pastors have tried to argue the case for themselves and their families, whether it be a salary increase or an increase in benefits. I have witnessed pastors make fools out of themselves trying to push their own personal agenda during budgeting time. I have served congregations my whole career that were always willing to take care of the pastor as best they could. All I had to do was let them know what my situation was and what my needs were. In almost every case that I have been a party to, I have witnessed God's people's strong desire to care for their pastor.

Ultimately, financial issues are the most controversial matters in the budget process in the voters assembly at the end of the fiscal year. But in our case, this is not true. Because the English District has a fiscal year ending on January 31 and beginning on February 1, it is often an opportunity for congregations to still involve themselves as they see what God would have for the life of His people. This is another argument for why congregations should consider moving to a fiscal year rather than a calendar year for budgeting and financial matters. A fiscal year not ending on December 31 allows for more flexibility from the congregation standpoint to deal with financial discrepancies, income and expense variations, and rising costs of other material things connected to the budget.

Pastoral Leaders Must Contribute to the Financial Life and Work of the Congregation

Stewardship is not something that pastors simply teach in Bible class or preach about in a sermon. Stewardship is a lifestyle that pastors must lead by example. Pastors must contribute financially to their congregations as an outflow of their stewardship to God and not as some kind of public display for their people. A pastoral leader cannot ask the people of God that he serves to be faithful in stewardship to God if he does not practice stewardship also. In my career, it has been a very simple principle that the people of God follow the leader in his actions, including matters of stewardship.

This question always becomes a difficult one when talking to pastors. I have had every range of excuses, explanations, and rationalizations as to why pastors don't financially contribute to the congregational ministry where they serve. One pastor told me that his stewardship was his service to the congregation as a pastor. He went on to say that he will not give financially to his congregation and that it was foolish for a pastor to do so. I don't think I need to go further with this story before the reader understands that that pastor and congregation quickly had problems upon his arrival. The laymen and women heard him say that and watched his actions; this led to frustration and anger on the part of many within the congregation.

The simple point for me regarding this topic is this: don't ask your people to give of themselves to the work of the church if you don't do it yourself. Leadership is all about leading by example and doing the difficult and tough things that you expect others to do for the sake of the ministry or congregation where you serve. Strong and faithful stewardship as a pastor will go a long way in teaching the people of God how to be good stewards. My mother and father never sat my brother, sister, and me down and lectured us about stewardship. We simply watched how they lived and what they did in their baptismal life of love for God and love for their neighbor. My parents did regularly tell us that the first check that they wrote when they received a paycheck was their stewardship offering to the church. This was the normal way of living for us, and it is the way that my siblings and I have grown up and live now.

Stewardship is a lifestyle and not a response to the situation at hand. Too often, financial matters within the church are looked at as a one-time event rather than a lifestyle or normalized way of living. Financial matters in the church are theological matters. Therefore, it is critically important for pastors to lead by example. Any financial matter within the congregation will always turn into, if it has not already, a theological matter that potentially will cause discord and frustration.

Conclusion

While the conversation about finances is not very popular among theologians, it is a very important element for pastoral leaders as they serve and guide the people of God. I fully realize that for many pastors, reading this chapter is not going to be the most enjoyable thing for them. However, it could be the difference between having success or not as a pastoral leader in a congregational setting today. Understanding the importance of finances and keeping the topic in a theological perspective are the tasks of the pastor as he leads the people of God in stewardship.

Understanding basic financial terms is important for any leader. This is especially true for pastoral leaders—having an understanding of what certain financial terms are will help the pastoral leader navigate the landscape of congregational or organizational leadership. While I do not expect any pastor to have a complete and full grasp of financial terminology or fiscal understanding, I do believe that every pastor must have a basic knowledge of matters like cash flow, budget, income, expense, and return on investments.

The budgeting process is stressful and difficult enough for the congregation and for the pastor as it is. Understanding how to effectively budget and effectively forecast income and expenses can assist in making the process less stressful and less difficult. While pastoral leaders ought to be fully and completely involved in the process, congregational leaders must take responsibility for the activity and the process itself. The pastor should never dominate or lead the process outright as the budgeting process occurs.

Over time, I have seen many congregations thrive as they have taken excess proceeds and invested them in an endowment-style account or simply in a money market or interest-bearing account. Congregations who understand the financial impact of being wise with excess cash tend to be successful in ministry operations because of an adherence to fiscal stewardship. Too often in my ministry, I have seen laity and pastors not understand the definition of a not-for-profit corporation. A not-for-profit corporation does not mean you do not generate profit. If you don't have the money, you can't carry out your mission. Therefore, being fiscally wise and investing proceeds that congregations have after expenses is not only wise; it is also fiscally sound.

Pastoral leaders must contribute financially to the work of the church and the ministry where they serve. Asking the people of God to be faithful stewards to the ministry or the mission without doing it yourself as a pastor is a recipe for disaster and hypocritical theologically. Pastors who lead by example have a higher likelihood of being successful in their parish as the people of God quickly build trust and respect for them as the pastoral leader. This naturally occurs when the leader does what he asks his people to do, rather than asking them to do things he is not willing to do himself.

REFLECTION

1. Consider Luke 14:25–33:

Now great crowds accompanied Him, and He turned and said to them, "If anyone comes to Me and does not hate his own father and mother and wife and children and brothers and sisters, yes, and even his own life, he cannot be My disciple. Whoever does not bear his own cross and come after Me cannot be My disciple. For which of you, desiring to build a tower, does not first sit down and count the cost, whether he has enough to complete it? Otherwise, when he has laid a foundation and is not able to finish, all who see it begin to mock him, saying, 'This man began to build and was not able to finish.' Or what king, going out to encounter another king in war, will not sit down first and deliberate whether he is able with ten thousand to meet him who comes against him with twenty thousand? And if not, while the other is yet a great way off, he sends a delegation and asks for terms of peace. So therefore, any one of you who does not renounce all that he has cannot be My disciple."

- Does your congregation count the cost before laying the foundations of the building?
- Do you have the mentality that some have had over the years: "No need to plan; God will provide"?

2. How do you or your congregation deal with the budget process each year?

3. Is there a process that is followed to ensure proper forecasting for income and expenses within your congregational setting?

4. Evaluate your congregation or personal stewardship based on the parable of the talents in Matthew 25:14–30:

For it will be like a man going on a journey, who called his servants and entrusted to them his property. To one he gave five talents, to another two, to another one, to each according to his ability. Then he went away. He who had received the five talents went at once and traded with them, and he made five talents more. So also he who had the two talents made two talents more. But he who had received the one talent went and dug in the ground and hid his master's money. Now after a long time the master of those servants came and settled accounts with them. And he who had received the five talents came forward, bringing five talents more, saying, "Master, you delivered to me five talents; here, I have made five talents more." His master said to him, "Well done, good and faithful servant. You have been faithful over a little; I will set you over much. Enter into the joy of your master." And he also who had the two talents came forward, saying, "Master, you delivered to me two talents; here, I have made two talents more." His master said to him, "Well done, good and faithful servant. You have been faithful over a little; I will set you over much. Enter into the joy of your master." He also who had received the one talent came forward, saying, "Master, I knew you to be a hard man, reaping where you did not sow, and gathering where you scattered no seed, so I was afraid, and I went and hid your talent in the ground. Here, you have what is yours." But his master answered him, "You wicked and slothful servant! You knew that I reap where I have not sown and gather where I scattered no seed? Then you ought to have invested my money with the bankers, and at my coming I should have received what was my own with interest. So take the talent from him and give it to him who has the ten talents. For to everyone who has will more be given, and he will have an abundance. But from the one who has not, even what he has will be taken away. And cast the worthless servant into the outer darkness. In that place there will be weeping and gnashing of teeth."

- Are you a faithful steward of the resources God has given to you?
- Do you bury your talents and live in fear of what will or may be?

CHAPTER X

Leadership as a Means of Pastoral Care

The role of a pastoral leader is and always will remain chiefly to be the one who gives the gifts of God in the forms of His Word and Sacraments. Though pastoral leadership encompasses many other aspects and avenues within the daily life of the congregation, being the voice of God and His instrument of distribution is what pastoral leadership is all about. This reality is one that will continue to remain the centerpiece of all that is discussed in pastoral leadership. In ordination, every pastor confesses that he will faithfully preach the Word of God and administer the Sacraments of Christ with fidelity and integrity. This is and will remain the chief role and function of all pastoral leaders now and into the future.

As I have the privilege of interacting with seminarians as a district president, I like to ask the same question to all fourth-year seminarians that I get into the district or that I encounter. The question that I ask them is very simple: What are you looking forward to when you are ordained and become a pastor? While the answers do vary, in almost every case, preaching, teaching, and administering the Sacraments are the chief things that the fourth-year seminarians tell me they are looking forward to after ordination and installation. It may seem like common sense to you that a seminarian would say this; however, I have received other answers to the question. Oftentimes those answers are indications of men who will struggle in the ministry. If your chief desire and greatest passion are not for preaching the Word of God and administering the Sacraments as a pastoral leader, you may consider entering a different career path. The Means of Grace that God has established are the preaching of the Word of God and administering His Sacraments. All other pastoral care flows from this reality and is connected to this reality.

Since pastoral care begins with and is all-encompassing of proclaiming the Word of God and administering His Sacraments, every facet of pastoral leadership is founded and rooted in this reality. There is no doubt in my mind that early on in my career I was able to quickly build trust with the people of God I served because I was dedicated to preaching, teaching, and administering the Sacraments. There is no greater place in the pastoral office to build respect, love, and trust with the people of God than when you visit them in their homes or at the hospital and bring them the Lord's Supper. It stands to reason that new seminarians entering the Office of the Public Ministry would desire to carry out the primary functions of the Office of the Holy Ministry. I believe firmly that pastoral leadership is an extension of the office of pastoral care.

Leadership Issues Are Spiritual Issues

Since pastoral leadership is pastoral care, all leadership issues are spiritual issues. I believe that every topic a pastoral leader encounters throughout his ministry and life will have some connective tissue to spiritual issues that he is having or that his people are having around him. Nothing within the congregational setting or the church at large stands alone without the assault of Satan as a mainstay and constant. Therefore, if you are having leadership issues, it stands to reason that those issues are likely generated in some way by a satanic influence to corrupt and cause difficulty in your life or the life of the parish. Too often as leaders, the natural compulsion for a pastor is the temptation to blame others when things do not go according to your plan. This is a temptation that becomes the default for pastoral leaders, especially when Satan has a grip on the life of the pastor, or the pastor has his eyes on other things than Christ alone.

When pastors speak of difficult situations of leadership, one of the most common areas centers around decision-making within congregational life. When I became a vicar in Brookings, South Dakota, at Our Savior Lutheran Church, they were in the middle of a building-addition project. I was excited and simultaneously fearful of the expectation that was placed upon me for the Lutheran Student Fellowship group that worked out of the church. This addition to the building was specifically for the students at South Dakota State University. I distinctly remember when I first arrived at vicarage my supervisor, Rev. Richard Townes, commented to me about not worrying about what the color of the carpet or the paint color in the bathroom of the addition was. These are not spiritual matters, and they are of no consequence to pastoral leadership. What he meant is that certain things are not spiritual in nature and therefore do not need to have pastoral leadership time invested into them. I have experienced many pastors who have wasted pastoral capital on frivolous things like paint color and carpet color and called it pastoral leadership.

Public communication to the congregation and community as a pastoral leader will be a defining hallmark of any effective leader and his legacy. Like Dr. Martin Luther of our Reformation heritage, we face the same unique challenge that pastors have faced throughout time and history: to communicate the Gospel effectively and clearly according to biblical standards. Like Luther, we must always understand the cultural audience to which we are speaking and clearly articulate the Word of God without fear or trepidation. Throughout my service as bishop, I have encountered many church leaders who are more concerned with being popular among their district congregations or parish memberships than with clearly and concisely articulating the Word of God and His commands.

Pastoral leaders who are afraid to be criticized because they fear losing popularity have created a spiritual problem within the congregation. Courage and bravery are traits that are exhibited only when necessary and are not traits that effective leaders simply walk around and flaunt. When pastoral leadership is hampered by fear, it will always give off an aura and impression that a lack of trust in Christ is normal. This will have a negative impact on your people and could lead them away from trusting in Christ alone and His grace. All the leadership issues that I have come across in my career as a pastor or as a district president and bishop are spiritual issues and must be dealt with accordingly.

We must not forget that lay leadership issues that come up are often spiritual issues within congregations. Recently, I was sitting at a council meeting of a congregation where I witnessed one of the lay leaders aggressively attacking another lay leader about a point that was insignificant and inconsequential. First, the man's behavior was totally out of line and not Christlike in loving his neighbor. Second, the point that was being made was unnecessary and could be considered totally out of line. In both cases and instances, I pointed out to the pastor the deep spiritual issues I believed existed within the life of that church council. It was not simply a matter of opinions that were different—it was a spiritual issue that divided the two who were arguing at the council meeting. Effective pastoral leaders must understand that when leadership issues cross over into spiritual issues, they must be dealt with accordingly and directly. That is why all leadership issues are spiritual issues and why pastoral leadership is a form of pastoral care.

Pastoral Leadership Is Word and Sacrament Leadership

One of the great joys of being in the Office of the Holy Ministry is the ability to proclaim the Word of God and administer His Sacraments faithfully to His people. What this means in practice is that pastoral leadership is Word-and-Sacrament leadership. Being ordained and installed to serve God's people in any given ministry sets you apart to be a pastoral leader. In ordination, many Scriptures are read to remind you of the role to which God has called you. This is laid out clearly in 1 Timothy 4:6–16:

> If you put these things before the brothers, you will be a good servant of Christ Jesus, being trained in the words of the faith and of the good doctrine that you

> have followed. Have nothing to do with irreverent, silly myths. Rather train yourself for godliness; for while bodily training is of some value, godliness is of value in every way, as it holds promise for the present life and also for the life to come. The saying is trustworthy and deserving of full acceptance. For to this end we toil and strive, because we have our hope set on the living God, who is the Savior of all people, especially of those who believe.
>
> Command and teach these things. Let no one despise you for your youth, but set the believers an example in speech, in conduct, in love, in faith, in purity. Until I come, devote yourself to the public reading of Scripture, to exhortation, to teaching. Do not neglect the gift you have, which was given you by prophecy when the council of elders laid their hands on you. Practice these things, immerse yourself in them, so that all may see your progress. Keep a close watch on yourself and on the teaching. Persist in this, for by so doing you will save both yourself and your hearers.

This passage from 1 Timothy lays out the foundational principles for all ordained pastors. Anyone standing in the Office of the Holy Ministry should heed the words, especially of 1 Timothy 4:16, "Keep a close watch on yourself and on the teaching. Persist in this, for by so doing you will save both yourself and your hearers." Everything that the pastor does reflects the commands of God and the proclamation of His will to His people. Therefore, being on guard with all that you do and say is in accord with the Word of God, and proclaiming Jesus Christ until He returns is both crucial and critical for any good pastoral leader. Keeping a watch on yourself and your teaching is a matter of good pastoral care and will help to set an example for the people you serve.

Teaching a proper understanding of the Sacrament of the Altar will always focus on the work Christ has done in His death and resurrection for the salvation of all mankind. Because of this reality, pastoral leaders must constantly watch what they say and how they say it as it pertains to the commands and promises of God. One of those biblical texts that is so comforting to the people of God that pastors should continually uphold as a means of understanding God's will in the life of His people is Ephesians 2:8–10, "For by grace you have been saved through faith. And this is not your own doing; it is the gift of God, not a result of works, so that no one may boast. For we are His workmanship, created in Christ Jesus for good works, which God prepared beforehand, that we should walk in them."

Proclaiming this Gospel reality sets forth what all pastoral leadership, and thus Word-and-Sacrament leadership, is all about. By clearly defining God's Word and administrating the Sacraments appropriately, pastors declare the forgiveness and work of Jesus Christ as a means of leading His people through a dark place in their lives and world. This reality is pointed out in John 8:12, "Again Jesus spoke to them, saying, 'I am the light of the world. Whoever follows Me will not walk in darkness, but will have the light of life.'" Jesus Christ is the light of the world, which makes all the proclamation of Christ from the pastoral office a means of leading.

Every aspect of pastoral ministry is centered around Word and Sacrament, making pastoral ministry and pastoral care the centerpiece of leading the people of God. Unfortunately, this is where many pastors today misinterpret both their call and the expectation from Christ. As Paul tells the pastors from Ephesus in Acts 20:28, shepherd the flock over which you have been placed as an overseer. Shepherding means many things, but it chiefly refers to providing safety, protection, and direction. All three of these functions are hallmarks of the pastoral office as we hear the commands of Christ to lead His people in Word and Sacrament ministry.

Leaving the Church Better Than You Received It

One of the key principles that I have learned from effective leaders throughout the time I have been in the ministry is simply this: leave the ministry you received better off than when you were given it. What this means to me is simple. I have often described this principle in my life as a pastor as stewarding the resources and gifts God has placed me in charge of as a trustee. I also believe it is a hallmark of any good pastoral leader as he seeks to care for the people of God given to him by Christ. When you enter a congregation or ministry, assess the health and wellness of the congregation or ministry you are serving. Work diligently for as long as you are a pastor or leader to grow and expand the ministry under your care. Whether you use financial metrics, attendance, Bible study or worship growth, or overall value, make it a goal when you leave the ministry to ensure that it is better than when you started.

This is applicable to overall congregational health and wellness as well as spiritual health and wellness. Some pastoral leaders have a unique ability to take spiritually struggling congregations and move them to spiritually healthy congregations. In some cases, you will come to congregations that are deprived of confessional subscription or biblical fidelity—you must ensure that before you leave that congregation or ministry, it is strengthened in its spiritual health and biblical fidelity. It is not simply good enough to preach without also teaching to advance the spiritual health and wellness of the congregation. To leave a congregation spiritually healthier than when you received it, you must identify the areas of theological weakness and expand the knowledge of the people in those areas.

Regarding finances, ensuring that congregations have stronger financial health and wellness after you leave is rarely a trait that most pastors care about when taking a call or starting a new job. I have only known one other pastor who places that goal on himself and the congregation when he starts pastoring a congregation. If you as a pastoral leader are going to make pastoral care a priority in your ministry, pastoral leadership will naturally flow toward financial health and wellness for the congregation. This is also in fulfillment of God's command to be good stewards in the Gospel of Matthew, as well as the exhortation in Luke to count the cost before you build. Making every financial decision from a deeply rooted stewardship mentality will assist in assuring a ministry is better off financially when you leave than when you start.

One specific area of congregational life that tends to be placed on the back burner with new pastors is the congregational structure. When first hearing the phrase "congregational structure," most pastors chuckle and ignore it. However, in some cases, congregational structures inhibit theological integrity and confessional adherence. If a congregation is more focused on structure and policy than it is on theological fidelity and biblical inerrancy, then difficulty between pastor and parish leaders can arise and be dramatic. Ensuring that congregational structure and biblical fidelity go hand in hand will assist in assuring that when you leave the ministry the next man who takes over will have a solid foundation and a strong base on which to build.

Iron Sharpens Iron

The biblical concept of iron sharpening iron is from Proverbs 27:17, "Iron sharpens iron, and one man sharpens another." When pondering this theological principle, I have always remembered the importance of high-quality pastoral leaders being my mentors, friends, and father confessors. It is crucial and important to understand that to fulfill Proverbs 27:17, you must seek out those who are high-quality pastoral leaders so that the concept of iron sharpening iron may occur. The simple beauty of this concept is that God provides us with other pastoral leaders to help sharpen and hone our pastoral leadership skills and personal awareness. Having a brother in Christ who can be your sharpening tool is a blessing and gift from God.

Throughout my career, I have been blessed with men who have helped to sharpen me in my role as pastor and as leader of the district. The one stark reality that everyone learns throughout the process of sharpening is it's not always comfortable; nor is it always easy. Oftentimes throughout my life when I am being sharpened by another man, it occurs when I don't want it to or in a corrective way that is humbling to me. During my early years in the parish, I remember having frustration both in my congregational life and in my personal career development within the pastoral ministry. It took a beloved brother and friend to sharpen me, one man to another, as I received loving rebuke and correction. I remember another instance when one of my beloved laymen in the congregation took me out to lunch and proceeded to sharpen me in a loving way regarding my passion and desire for leadership. These events combined to fulfill the Proverbs 27 concept of iron sharpening iron. I am thankful and joyful that God provided other men to sharpen me at moments in my life when my leadership was dull and ineffective. Pray that God provides you with other men to be a sharpening tool for you as a pastoral leader as you carry out your pastoral care for the people of God.

Since pastoral leadership is pastoral care, being sharpened as a pastor is not only something you should desire, it is also a privilege that God has provided. It is incumbent upon you to receive the sharpening of a brother in love and care rather than from a critical heart or a critical mindset. This likewise is what the Eighth Commandment, "You shall not give false testimony against your neighbor," is referencing. Luther's definition of this commandment in the Small Catechism exhorts all of us to put the best construction on everything. One pointed example of this occurs in the installation service of a new pastor in a congregation. The officiant asks this question to the congregation: "Will you honor and uphold your pastor as he serves Christ in all his God-pleasing responsibilities? Will you aid him as he cares for his family? Will you be diligent to 'put the best construction on everything,' recognizing that 'love covers a multitude of sins'?" (*LSB Agenda*, p. 169). This question that the congregation answers in installation services reminds us that putting the best construction on everything is an act of love and demonstrates pastoral care.

Throughout my time as a district president and bishop, it has become clear to me that sometimes iron sharpening iron occurs against the will of the pastoral leader. What I mean by that is that I have witnessed many circumstances where pastors have been doing things that require a change in behavior, and the only way that that occurs is when discipline is given. Sometimes iron sharpens iron even when we aren't expecting it to. I have also witnessed other occasions where men have realized that the circumstances surrounding their situation were far more impactful to them than they first thought. We all learn at different speeds and at different paces. Because of this reality, we can be sharpened as pastoral leaders at moments in time that we are not even paying attention or expecting to be sharpened. There are many instances in my pastoral ministry where I looked back and realized that God was sharpening me despite my desire not to be sharpened. He allowed things to occur in order to knock rough edges off of my pastoral leadership style and performance. The beauty of Proverbs 27:17 is clearly the beauty that iron sharpens iron and one man sharpens another in his skills and pastoral care. This is a gift from God, and we ought to cherish it.

Setting Goals for Ministry

Since we've established clearly that pastoral care and pastoral leadership are one and the same, it stands to reason that good pastoral leaders will set goals in ministry. Throughout my time as a district president, I have heard from some very good pastors that applications from the business world have no place in the church. However, I would argue that good pastoral care, which is pastoral leadership, can utilize business verbiage and techniques for success and sustainability. One of those business techniques is goal-setting for congregational stability and growth. Desiring congregational health and wellness is one thing, and it's important to the life of the parish. It is entirely another thing to put into practice a plan to have congregational stability.

One of the goal-setting processes in good business leadership is doing a SWOT analysis. The word *SWOT* stands for the following:

1. ***S****trengths*: What are the things that your ministry or congregation does very well?

2. ***W****eaknesses*: What improvements does the congregation need? Or in what areas can improvements be made?

3. ***O****pportunities*: What are the areas that the congregation has not yet identified or ventured into?

4. ***T****hreats*: What are the areas that could cause the congregation to struggle or falter?

Goals for any ministry should be based on evaluating the strengths, weaknesses, opportunities, and threats that its congregation faces. Without doing a thorough SWOT analysis, congregations can waste time as they seek to do better ministry for the sake of the Gospel. But congregations that do go through a SWOT analysis process can identify those areas in ministry where they could improve and/or expand. By taking the time to evaluate the current health and wellness of the congregation or ministry you are serving, you can more effectively help that congregation or ministry set goals for congregational health and wellness.

One specific area that needs focused attention from the pastoral leader is the spiritual health and wellness of the congregation. Congregations can fall into a pattern that is highlighted by simply and only focusing on the Sunday morning worship service and quickly ignoring the other aspects that contribute to overall congregational strength. Effective and strong pastoral leadership will continually evaluate the spiritual health of the congregational ministry where you serve. For some pastoral leaders, this reality can be the differentiating factor between success and failure in ministry. Congregations that become unstable spiritually can be breeding grounds for false theology and evil behaviors. Making spiritual health and wellness a goal, and working toward the success of that goal, should be a priority for any effective pastoral leader.

Another area where goal-setting is important for effective pastoral leadership is in the realm of financial health and wellness. Every successful congregation that I have been a part of as a district president or as a pastor focused on being good stewards of the gifts that God had provided the ministry or the congregation. Financial health and wellness do not just occur within the life of a congregation or a ministry. Financial health and wellness only occur after dedicated planning and efforts are placed on the topic itself. This requires significant effort on the part of the pastoral leader and the members of the congregational leadership team.

Assuming that financial health and wellness will simply occur because it's a desire of the pastor is foolish and can be significantly detrimental to the ministry. It is my strong recommendation for any successful strong pastoral leader that they continuously make themselves aware of the spiritual, financial, and congregational wellness as a means of leading God's people.

Conclusion

Since pastoral leadership is pastoral care and the chief duty of the pastor is to proclaim the Word of God and administer His Sacraments, then all aspects of the pastoral ministry are tightly woven together and important. We cannot separate pastoral leadership from pastoral care in any way and must always connect them to the public proclamation of the Gospel and the administration of the Sacraments. Without pastoral care, you cannot have pastoral leadership within the life of a congregation.

In almost every case where a problem has occurred in the ministry that I have served or congregations I have supervised as bishop and president, all circumstances came down to spiritual problems rather than physical ones. Spiritual problems within the life of a congregation can be extremely disruptive and detrimental to ministry. Pastoral leaders must continually be on guard and monitor the spiritual health of the congregation or ministry that they are serving. Moments of spiritual conflict can lead to dramatic and real problems within the life of the ministry. Constant prayer before God to send the Holy Spirit to help maintain healthy spiritual members is an important task for every pastoral leader.

One of the greatest responsibilities that a pastor can have is admittance to the Lord's Table. Strong and effective pastoral leaders understand that Word-and-Sacrament ministry is the pinnacle of all that they will do as parish pastors. The altar of God and the rail of Holy Communion are the seats of the two most important functions and activities for all pastoral leaders. Disconnecting the strong bond between the administration of the Sacraments and the proclamation of the Word can be a critical error in the life of any pastoral leader.

It has always been my goal from the beginning of my ministry to leave a congregation or ministry healthier and stronger than the day that I started working there. This means everything that you do as a pastor or leader should build on moving the ministry forward and strengthening all aspects of the congregation or ministry where you serve as a pastoral leader. Any good pastor will have as a ministry goal leaving the ministry or congregation stronger than when he took over. This is important and is a part of the growth process for any pastor and ministry or congregation throughout their life cycle.

Since being introduced to the concept of iron sharpening iron, it has always intrigued me and motivated me. Seeking those strong, influential brothers to help mentor and sharpen one's pastoral skills is something that all new pastors should endeavor toward. The biblical concept of iron sharpening iron and one man sharpening another man toward the skill sets that God has given them is undervalued in our church today. It is a concept that more pastors should spend time on and develop within the life of their ministry and those around them. You are never too young or old to be sharpened by the Word of God and your brothers in your ministry life. Do not become overconfident that you as a pastoral leader do not need to be sharpened.

Finally, while business techniques and verbiage are not always welcomed in congregational ministry today, I believe it is important to set goals and evaluate ministry health and wellness. Continuous improvement only occurs when goals are set and measured along the ministry's life and leadership trajectory. It is not enough to desire health and wellness. It will only occur if it is planned and acted on. Do not be lulled into believing that positive things in ministry life simply happen without action and activity.

REFLECTION

1. Has your congregation or ministry performed a SWOT analysis recently?

2. What are some specific ways that you can seek out a mentor and/or a brother in Christ who can help sharpen you according to God's Word?

3. How can you help your ministry prepare to be better today than it was when you started or took over in the congregation or ministry you are serving?

4. What are some ways that your laity can help be more involved in the success and wellness of the parish or ministry where you serve?

5. Spend time discussing Proverbs 27:17, "Iron sharpens iron, and one man sharpens another." What does this mean in the life of your ministry or your congregation?

6. What are you doing to plan for success and sustainability within the life of the ministry or congregation where you serve?

CHAPTER XI

Conclusion

I would like to conclude this book at the very same place where I began it. For me, pastoral leadership is pastoral care, and as such, pastoral leadership centers around faithfully and boldly giving the gifts that are from God—namely, His Word and Sacraments—to His people. To be an effective pastoral leader means you must also be an effective pastoral caregiver to the people placed under your care. Pastoral leadership and pastoral care should never be separated or thought of differently since they both are concerned with the sheep of the great shepherd Jesus Christ. A wise layman once told me it's all about grace and that grace flows from Jesus Christ alone to His people.

I fully realize that many other things could be discussed in a work such as this. I have had this passion to write this book for many years, and the topics within it are merely a glimpse into the pastoral care and pastoral leadership experiences that I have had, both as a parish pastor and a district president. I have been overly blessed throughout my years of ministry to have high-quality pastoral leaders and high-quality lay leaders influence and teach me about what it means to be effective in the pastoral office as a pastoral leader. Any good pastor will recognize that those who have contributed to his formation are just as important as the gifts that God has provided him and the abilities that he has today.

This book is intended to be a helpful resource and a guide for discussion for lay leaders and pastors alike. The topics we have covered are those that have risen to the highest priority levels within my pastoral life and leadership life within the church. Many of these topics are directly drawn from the experiences that I have had as a parish pastor or as a district president. Over my time and service in the church, I have had unbelievable lay examples of faithfulness and leadership. It is also true that over my career I have had a few examples of what not to do in leadership and what not to be like as a layperson in the congregation. All of these experiences have helped to shape my outlook on the ministry and being a leader within the greater Church.

Examples of Biblical Leaders

Throughout the course of the biblical narrative, we can see various and different leadership styles of the people that God used to care for and lead His people. This has both a positive and a negative side to having so many leaders. The positive side is clearly that God can use various and different skill sets to accomplish the work of leading His people and caring for His Church. The biblical narrative helps to point out those varying and different leadership styles and how the people received those various styles. The negative aspect of this is that some of the leadership styles in the Bible demonstrate the things that we should not do in leadership rather than those things that are helpful in leadership. From Adam and Eve until Jesus came, biblical leadership has struggled under the weight and responsibility of caring for God's people.

The other significant point here is that Satan will do all that he can to destroy and disrupt the leadership of those specially called into the Office of the Holy Ministry. It is clear to me throughout my years of service in the parish and in the district that Satan works overtime on those called to lead God's Church. The immense pressure to live the baptismal life and resist the temptations of Satan is not minimized after you take your oath of ordination. Pastoral leaders are sinful human people as well and are prone to make mistakes from time to time. This reality must be remembered by anybody who is being led by a pastor. It also is in fulfillment with the Eighth Commandment, where Luther in the Small Catechism encourages us to put the best construction on everything.

I believe it is very healthy for anybody in leadership, especially those in pastoral leadership, to look to the biblical characters and to associate their leadership style with one of the leading biblical characters. Aspiring to be like a strong biblical leader is not a negative thing in the life of the church. While we will not be like Moses, Peter, Paul, or Jesus, we must strive to put our best foot forward, understanding whom we are serving and why we are serving. As shepherds of the Good Shepherd's flock, we must remain vigilant to ward off the wolves who come to seek and destroy the flock.

Final Word

Jesus says, "I am the way, and the truth, and the life. No one comes to the Father except through Me" (John 14:6). This is the centerpiece of all pastoral leadership and pastoral care: proclaiming Jesus Christ as the Savior of the world and the only mediator between God and men. It is a simple joy and honor to be able to lead the people of God. In my experience and throughout my ministry, I can tell you unequivocally that there have been many more high points and joys than low points and frustrations. Just as in the story of Moses, God will provide us with all that we need to supply us where our deficiencies occur. Do not be frustrated or overwhelmed, because Christ has promised to be with us to the very end of the age. Pastoral leadership and pastoral care are very rewarding lifestyles, and my encouragement is always to see the joy and benefit in serving rather than the burden.

Acknowledgments

There are certainly many people who deserve to be acknowledged in this book. Let me begin by acknowledging and thanking my wife and children. Wendy, Noah, Nathaniel, and Naomi have been very supportive throughout my years as a pastor, especially when I continued my education for my second master's and my doctorate. Likewise, they have been very understanding during my time as bishop and president whenever I have to spend a significant amount of time with visitations and congregational support meetings. It makes my job much easier knowing that my family is as dedicated to what I do as I am myself. We face challenges often; however, we continue to rely on and trust in our Lord and His grace in our lives.

I want to thank my sainted father, Dan, who during his earthly life taught me that leadership is more about what you do than what you say. I remember many days as a young boy going through our church clinging to his leg as we checked the doors throughout the building without turning lights on. My father's clear and calm demeanor rubbed off on me as I got older. I watched my mother and father as they taught my sister, brother, and me about faith and life in the church. What this meant for my siblings and me was a faith life that was deeply rooted within our church. Our faith life was not independent of the rest of our life—it was our entire life. For that, I am eternally grateful to both my parents.

From my early youth to this day, extended family has proved important to me and my faith life. Faith in my extended family is generational and has had a tremendous impact on me and my entire family. Going way back to my great-grandparents on my dad's side and my great-grandmother on my mother's side, I had strong examples of faith and life regularly shown to me. Throughout my whole life, I have been blessed with aunts and uncles, cousins, and other relatives who themselves have been faithful to God in the church. This is a tremendous blessing to me, and I give thanks to God for this reality.

For me, there is no doubt that second only to my father, my parish pastor, the sainted Rev. Dr. Ralph Fischer, had the single greatest impact on me and who I am as a leader today. I witnessed a pastor who held to biblical fidelity and scriptural integrity while all along loving his people and dedicating his life to serving and leading the church. I have built on this great foundational example throughout my entire pastoral career. Many small life lessons have been taught to me by my pastor from my youth. I am much of who I am as a clergyman today because of Ralph Fischer, as well as other beloved clergies in my life.

While there are too many to name one by one, I will mention a few other people who, throughout my career and educational life, have imprinted on me and helped me become who I am as a pastoral leader. As a student at Concordia University Wisconsin, I was significantly influenced by Dr. James Juergensen, Dr. Timothy Maschke, and coach Bret Corner. While at the seminary, I also had several influential people in my life, such as Dr. Larry Rast, Dr. David Scaer, Dr. Art Just, and Dr. Dan Gard. All these educators helped shape me as a pastor as well as a pastoral leader. Again, there are too many people to name, but I would like to say thank you to all who have had an impact on me as a student, a pastor, a teacher, and a friend.

One specific person who is owed a public thank-you is Mr. Keith Frndak. Over the last twenty-three years, I have sat at the feet of one of the greatest leaders in The Lutheran Church—Missouri Synod and learned what it is like to put faith and life together as a leader in the church. Keith has always been very gracious with his time, his input, and his care for me as a church worker and a leader in the greater church. Many of the positive habits that I have in leadership come from emulating Keith and what he has been able to do at Concordia Lutheran Ministries. I am eternally grateful for all the positive faithfulness and leadership examples that Keith has been able to give me. Much of what this book talks about in terms of leadership behavior was learned as I watched Keith throughout my years at Concordia Lutheran Ministries.

Last and certainly not least, I would like to extend my gratitude to Concordia Publishing House for trusting me to put together this work on leadership for the benefit of the Church and the Gospel message. Likewise, I would like to thank all those on staff at CPH who have put time into editing and producing this book. Partnership in the Gospel is something that we should not take for granted, and I am truly thankful for all those who have had input and physical help with this work.

Let me conclude by saying thanks to God our Father for the gifts that He has provided to me, both in life and in service to the Church. It is a humbling experience when you use the gifts and talents that God gives you for the sake of service to the Kingdom. I am fully aware that any positive impact or success I have had in my leadership life within the church is strictly and solely a gift from God in an immense amount of mercy on His part. I thank my heavenly Father for the faith given to me in Holy Baptism by the power and hand of the Holy Spirit.